What is Zija? What is in Zija? What is Moringa?

A Business and Health Singularity

Max Hailey

What is Zija? What is in Zija? What is Moringa?

Copyright © 2013 by Max Hailey

Business and Health Profiles Publications 2013

ISBN-13: 978-1483939827

ISBN-10: 1483939820

All rights reserved. No part of this book may be reproduced or transmitted in any form or by any means without written permission of the author.

Table of Contents

Introduction 1

Minting Opportunities in the Wellness Industry 3

Wellness: More than a Trend 5

Wellness and the Answer to Our Health Crisis 13

The Distribution of Wellness 17

The Secrets behind Distribution 19

Direct Marketing 23

Moringa Oleifera – The Modern Ambrosia 29

Cultivating Moringa 35

Getting Started with Network Marketing Right – the Lifeblood of making Money 39

Super-Secret Tip: Outsource your Social Media campaign. What is outsourcing? 55

What kind of business is best for you? 57

The 3 T's of Success 63

A closer look at Moringa and Zija 69

How Zija's is Helping People Achieve Their Financial Dreams 79

Earning Wealth with Zija using the right Network Marketing strategies 85

Bottom Line on Zija Products: 103

Conclusion 107

Introduction

To literally millions of people, the concept of making passive and constant flow of income is absolutely foreign. Have you ever asked yourself this simple question – What are the top network marketers doing different? How are they earning so much at such a rapid rate, while for others it is like pulling teeth to just find someone interested enough to hear them out? It is easy to find hundreds of thousands of resources that will inform you of age-old strategies. It does not come as a surprise that these 'age-old' strategies do not work. You need to be current with the changing technology.

What will be discussed next will open the Pandora box of making passive money. Do you have a hobby? Did you know that you could earn money by educating people about something not known to anyone yet something, which exists since a long time and have touched the lives of millions? Once you have the basics right, you can just sit back and watch money flow.

Are you visiting a place sunnier than Iceland on a holiday? Don't worry; you can even make money while you are enjoying the weather on vacation.

This book will walk you through the insides of an industry that never sees recession – wellness! And you don't need to be from a health and fitness background. The idea behind this book is turnkey that means you can start immediately.

Who should read this book?

You, you, and you! Well, an audience for this book has not been identified as anyone who wishes to make a lifelong income should read this book. Essentially, this book will be helpful to two distinct groups of people...

People Interested in making money

People CONSIDERING alternative ways to make money

So let's cut to the chase, and look ahead to tomorrow and start promoting products that "WILL BE HOT" not just tomorrow, but for the life time of each user, resulting in huge profits today, tomorrow and for your children.

Enjoy!

Minting Opportunities in the Wellness Industry

The wellness industry is booming throughout the globe. It doesn't matter, which part of the world is hit by recession – the wellness industry is recession proof. In this chapter, we will talk about the wellness industry. We will also talk about Moringa Oleifera and its influence towards an unstoppable market.

Stating that wellness is the 'next big' thing is an understatement. Wellness is a holistic term, which helps any individual rethink about their body, mind, and spirit, and how it influences their health. Wellness is a multi-dimensional term. Ignoring any of the elements of wellness will mar the potential of remaining happy and truly healthy. Matter of fact, failing to take care of wellness will put you at disadvantage, especially if you're under the impression the government will take care of you.

Our daily life is affected by Wellness in many ways. By adapting to a healthy lifestyle, you are committing yourself to different ways than you were once used to. You will think twice before your mouth starts watering when you lay eyes on that greasy burger. Instead, you will assess that burger carefully against other choices; healthier choices. You will see the difference vis a vis increased energy, lost weight, and an overall feeling of well-being and awesomeness. If you continue to mar your decision making with poor lifestyle choices such as a donut instead of apple, you will feel fatigue, suffer from obesity, and find yourself quick to get sick.

Baby Boomers, Patients, Consumers, Generation X, and anyone who has a brief idea about the meaning of 'healthy' are stepping on the ladder of Wellness. Wellness and preventive care go hand in hand where the motive is to prevent getting sick before anything happens.

People are seeing much more sense in "Prevention is better than cure" instead of spending a fortune on treatment. This has ushered a new era; one, which focuses on preventive care and medicine.

Wellness: More than a Trend

Wellness is more than a trend. Rather, it is a lifestyle change. It is important to note that this era depends on the new industry and market for support. The wellness industry was incepted decades ago when it was difficult for subscribers to find a place to buy healthy alternatives as compared to overly processed food.

With the Wellness industry coming to the lime light, more and more businesses, store fronts, and food establishment came to the center stage to meet the demands of this lifestyle change. This doesn't mean that the market is saturated and that there is no room for new businesses. Matter of fact, the Wellness industry is growing rapidly, which means there are plenty of opportunities for those who are prepared to leverage it.

Wellness has five characteristics that will ensure its continued survival.

Affordability

While at the outset of the wellness trend, products and services were not available to meet the increasing demand and they were definitely not affordable. Thanks to new technology and manufacturing capabilities, these products have become more effective, efficient, and affordable. And the irony – these prices are astronomically dropping to make these products and services more and more affordable.

Today, these wellness products and services are becoming more affordable to the masses including families with low income. This is due to the fact that massive retail giants and other restaurants are offering healthier alternatives that were traditionally unhealthy.

Legs

This element simply means that the wellness products and services take shorter duration to move from the shelf after advertisements and promotions to the end customer. However, it should be well understood that wellness is a state, which cannot be packaged easily.

The best part about the industry is that once these advertisements and endorsements stop airing, the significance of wellness does not waver off from the minds of the audience. Instead, it penetrates deep within their conscience and promises them a lifestyle that they had desired.

Moreover, the government adds to the wellness trends as they are concerned with the rising cost of health care at a local, regional, and national level. They understand that a small amount of prevention can save millions of dollars in treatment and care.

This is the reason why a sizeable spend yearly on Wellness, health, and prevention will transform the mindset of wellness to more than fad or trend to a life style. This is 'free advertising' for those in the Wellness area.

Continual Consumption

A product or trend usually lasts even after the supply meets the consumer's demands once they purchase it. For wellness industry, this trait is evident through vitamins and other healthy food alternatives. Once a person is determined about living a wellness lifestyle, they are bound to commit themselves to purchasing the requisite items for dieting, exercising, and items used for preventive medicine.

Once this positive life style switch is imbibed in a person, it creates a great platform for those marketing wellness products.

Universal Appeal

Wellness has not only attracted a niche crowd but everyone everywhere. It has created a universal appeal, one that attracts people irrespective of their age, gender, race, or background. It is of prime importance to people especially in today's unhealthy environment when sickness and illness are one step away.

Entrepreneurs see this as an opportunity to provide services to the millions of potential customers, which has made the Wellness industry almost recession proof and most sought after to enter into.

A Quick Consumption Time

Wellness products have low shelf life, in it they have to be consumed quickly and in a short amount of time. In order to get the most out of wellness products and services, they must be accessed quickly.

These five elements will create a long lasting effect on the public. Wellness products and services must have all these three critical elements to hold their place in the minds of the consumers. Therefore, for those who are considering entering into the Wellness industry, they need to consider if the product or service they wish to make available, sell, or promote has these elements, period.

At the end, irrespective of what you choose remember that Wellness has created a mark around the globe. It is here to stay and will remain fresh.

Other factors that make Wellness a viral industry

The wellness industry has been booming throughout the globe. It doesn't matter, which part of the world is hit by recession – wellness industry is recession proof. In this chapter, we will talk about the wellness industry. We will also talk about Moringa Oleifera and its influence towards an unstoppable market.

The wellness movement is omnipresent and contagious. Yes, contagious! When we see our friend enjoy the benefits of a healthy lifestyle, we are susceptible to imitate that change to benefit from that effect. This has made wellness a 'must have' which drives more consumers to seek products and services that help them with the desired results.

Let us take an example. Alice leads a healthy lifestyle. She starts going to yoga and begins to eat healthy food instead of greasy burgers and sitting in front of a TV all day. One day, you see how fit, happy, and healthy Alice is. You are tempted to adapt to that life style and reap the benefits you are seeing for yourself. You start going to Yoga and decide to make the required lifestyle choices. You see these are viral trends and attract a person to live a healthy lifestyle.

What Has Made Wellness So Desirable?

So why is wellness so sought after? What makes it so attractive? Despite the obvious benefits of health and feeling good, wellness is more than just a trend; it is a lifestyle chance, one that has committed people for lifetime. That alone makes this industry attractive, especially for those who wish to become entrepreneurs.

Our society moved away from true Wellness decades ago with the advent of quick and easy meals and technological advancements that made many tasks in life easier. Instead of walking to work, we simply drive. Instead of pushing a hand mower to cut the grass, we sit in style and comfort driving a gas fueled mower. Instead of slow cooking, we 'nuke' processed, packaged and prepared foods. All these seemingly minor changes to how we do things have created a society of perpetual laziness and demand for the fast, the easy, the here and now.

There are a few factors that help to contribute to the modern day need for a strong Wellness industry.

Economy and Health

Obesity is an evil that has serious concerns today. It is estimated that over 65% of the population in the United States is obese. This is a dramatic increase from decades ago before the advent of fast food; laziness perpetuated by modern technology, and processed prepackaged meals that contain more salt than nutrition.

There now exists a new discrimination, one that is perhaps more powerful and more pervasive then race, color, or gender; that new discrimination is based on wealth and health. Often we look at obese people and compare them with the poor while the rich are supposed to be similar to sticks and twigs. However, we do not remember the fact that obesity was once a sign of the wealthy and the rich. Henry VIII was very fat and rich man. However, obesity is no longer associated with the wealthy. Rather, it is the other way around. Why is this? More people today suffer from obesity then hunger. This is the first time in history, and when one considers the billions of people on the plant, it is simply staggering.

It is interesting to note that our society is now taking responsibility and wishes to avoid obesity at all cost. They are more conscious about healthy choices. In perspective, consumers prefer to choose quick and easy over healthy alternatives. Why stand in the kitchen creating a healthy meal of a fresh salad and seasoned baked chicken when you can easily run out to the store for a prepackaged microwavable meal or, if you are really lazy, ride to the fast food outlet and go through the drive thru lane for a unhealthy greasy burger and salty fries. The home cooked meal is obviously the healthier choice, but millions fail to make the healthy choice, instead opting for fast food and microwave meals.

This leads many to a life of illness, fatigue, obesity, and a cycle of bad choices. The disparity between health and wealth is only perpetuated by our current disease based healthcare system where only the richest of the population can enjoy the benefits of physicians and adequate treatment for ailments and harmful conditions. This leaves low income individuals unable to treat the ailments and conditions that occur due to their continued bad lifestyle choices while the rich and wealthy are able to receive treatments and needed medication to counteract a bad diet and poor choices.

It is not about the views of others. Being overweight and unhealthy detriments a person's life. Every phase of our lives from finding a job to getting into a relationship to being active to perform day to day activities get negatively impacted by poor health and obesity. You are viewed as poor and uneducated if you do not get a quick remedy for this. Even if you are in the appropriate weight range, you will still be viewed as unhealthy since you take poor diet.

Due to our disease based healthcare system, people are often told to accept malnutrition, headaches, fatigue, and other ailments as ordinary. This makes it a common trend to pay a visit to drug store.

Junk Food and McDiets

Today, the food industry is targeting low income families with junk food and unhealthy products. It is a dark mark to the wellness industry. These processed foods have ingredients and other chemicals that are far from nutritional. While it is up to you to see what is right and what is not, there is a disparity in proper education about Wellness and preventive medicine.

What's more, these foods are chemically designed to have a potato chip effect on your body so you cannot eat just one. If you ate a few apples or a banana or two you will soon move on to another type of food, maybe a carrot or an orange. However, it is hard to satisfy yourself with a burger and few fries.

The Wellness industry has leaned that it should be designing products to take advantage of this by offering healthier, easy alternatives to harmful foods and diets. Many restaurants are actually offering healthier menu alternatives but many of these establishments are offering too little too late.

The Sickness Industry

For the medical industry and healthcare field there is much money to be made when people are sick. Understanding how the current healthcare system works will go a long way in helping you establish a presence in the Wellness market and industry. Part of the modern Wellness movement is altering how we view healthcare. Our current healthcare system is driven by profit instead of the wellbeing of patients. Almost every sector of the healthcare industry is driven by profit gained by keeping you sick. The current line of thinking for much of the medical industry is that we are sick due to bad genes or perhaps even bad luck. In reality it is our lifestyle choices that often determine if we get sick. It is time to realize this and work toward change. As you change your attitude and lifestyle; you will then be able to help others to change.

Let us take a look briefly at the pharmaceutical industry and how their desire for a quick profit dictates the treatments you receive. Often the medication you receive may not be the best possible medication available. It is at the discretion of your physician which medication to prescribe to you. Now, there are ethical doctors and pharmaceutical companies that do actually have your best interest in mind, but sadly most are driven, by law, to create profits for their shareholders as their first priority.

It is highly likely that you are at a doctor's place due to poor lifestyle. The constant ill health that you suffer from and are seeking relief for may be the result of a condition you could've avoided in the first place by adhering to Wellness. You can easily eliminate the need for medication by changing your habits.

This means that stress reduction activities such as massage, yoga, and even acupuncture can have amazing results when applied to your headache. Prescriptions do not come cheap, which is leading many patients and consumers to what they see as alternative preventive treatments. These alternative preventive treatments have been in play for many centuries by other cultures, in fact, many Wellness programs have claimed them as 'proven to work'. We will talk about Moringa later as an example.

People are wondering if America's healthcare system is so bad off that it hurts more than it helps? Preventive care and Wellness, however, makes more sense so you can avoid unnecessary medications and hospital trips all together.

Wellness and the Answer to Our Health Crisis

There is now a need for healthier alternatives to the more traditional treatment options that we have been conditioned to turn to. Instead of seeking treatment after the onset of disease, much of the population is seeing the benefits of preventive medicine and care.

This has created a need in the market place ripe for the picking for those that have enough foresight to participate in the opportunity. There are several areas of the Wellness industry that one can benefit from both health wise and monetary wise. Remember, venturing into Wellness by establishing a business or taking advantage of an opportunity will result in helping those truly in need through education and providing them with affordable and available Wellness products and services.

The idea is to identify where in this industry exists the biggest potential for greatest growth. This will give you an indication where to invest your money and efforts to obtain the right return on investment.

There are two primary areas of the Wellness industry that you can harness for your own business: Wellness foods and Wellness medicine.

The Economics of Food and Opportunities for Wellness Business

So why is the current state of the food industry deteriorating? Blame it on competition! Yes, really. A few decades back, technology allowed food manufacturers to process food products quickly and easily; businesses were competing with each other to determine who can sell the most in the shortest duration. In light of this competition, manufacturers only focused on the taste of food rather than its nutritious value. Essentially, no one was aware that consuming mindless amount of fatty, salty and sugared food would decrease the quality of life. What is worse, the process used for storage and preservation of food destroys the original vitamins that exist in a food item. Net-net, the end result of this manufacturing process is food with little or no nutritional value.

There is clearly a fantastic opportunity for you to offer the population a way to purchase healthy foods. We are talking about food that is not overly processed, loaded with preservatives, and offer nothing but taste. There is a misconception that healthy food is bland. Healthy food can also be flavorful and amazing. All that consumers need to know are the alternatives available.

By offering wellness products that are rich in nutrition yet delicious will help you to get an edge over the others because you are filling a gap they have missed in the past. Food is the building block of our body and not just a catalyst for our taste buds.

Wellness, Food and You

As wellness continues to become the key focus area, food manufacturers are striving to correct the mistakes they have made in the past especially how they manufacture and produce food items. If you are looking at starting a business in the wellness industry, the time is ripe so you should act now.

The growing, harvesting, and transporting of food and educating the consumers on the benefits of healthy food are the areas in high demand yet there are only a few who can meet this demand.

Often, Americans blame the U.S. government for the current state of the food industry. However, truth be told, the government did not fail the people due to an ill intent rather through outdated programs.

Where Knowledge is Power

It is important to understand that knowledge in itself is a commodity. If it is new to the masses, it is generally high priced. ConsumerLab.com is one such company, which felt the need to provide knowledge around wellness products.

The site was founded with a motive to provide information related to vitamins and supplement to the consumers. It is a known fact that there are various loopholes in the regulation, which is often taken advantage of from unscrupulous manufacturers. These manufacturers take advantage of consumer ignorance and provide subpar and harmful products to them.

As a result, many individuals are left with the idea that all vitamins and supplements are either harmful or simply fail to work. Ask yourself, do you believe that vitamins work to improve health? If you don't, then you were probably one of the victims of unethical companies peddling poor quality vitamins.

Common problems with these vitamins and supplements are:

• These vitamins or supplements contain harmful chemicals.

• These vitamins simply do not contain what they are supposed to.

• These vitamins fail to release their ingredients because of a poor manufacturing process.

ConsumerLab.com took it upon them to test vitamins and supplements for the consumer market. The company then rates the products and provides a description about the product and how well it works.

For consumers this knowledge is invaluable. In this scenario, ConsumerLab.com provided consumers not with new technology but with information. This information is invaluable for the consumer wanting to make the best possible decision about their Wellness. Information and knowledge is just as valuable as Wellness products and services like yoga, exercise, and meditation.

Without honest assessment of wellness products, consumers can never stay in the state of wellness. By enlightening the consumers about Wellness, you will create a very strong consumer base.

The Distribution of Wellness

Those who are interested in making money (and who isn't?) probably know by now that the "secret" to success doesn't necessarily lie in imitating those who have already made a fortune, but rather in finding a strategy that, while based in the same fundamental principles, will work for you and your particular strengths and interests. So far, this chapter has talked about the potential of cashing in on the Wellness revolution by understanding the need for high quality products and working to develop and manufacture those products (such as supplements or Wellness-promoting foods). However, it is plain that this is not everyone's forte. If this is the case with you, do not despair, there are still other opportunities through which you can make your fortune within the Wellness trend.

Consider, for instance, what might be possible if your core business strength lies not in creating and developing, but rather in exposing products to others. Being good at exposing new products is a strength that the Wellness revolution sorely needs, because without such people providing this valuable service, the average person will never be aware of the availability of these Wellness promoting products and how they could change his or her life. In other words, even though manufacturing is a vitally important part of business, it is nothing without distribution in place to get the products to people who wish to purchase them.

In fact, it has been written that distribution may well be the more critically important side of the coin in this matter. If nothing else, it is the easier discipline to master, and the one over which people tend to have more direct control. Those who develop products for sale are ultimately at the mercy of market trends; they must anticipate the next major trends that will occur within a particular consumer demographic and then develop products that will appeal to that trend in a high quality way. On the other hand, distribution is a more consistent effort. While the nature of distribution does change over time, the truth remains that it is fundamentally less volatile than manufacturing, such that consistent success can be achieved simply by focusing on distribution and "distributing the ever-expanding production of cutting-edge technology".

In other words, you need not develop or create products yourself to make a fortune in Wellness; you can simply choose to distribute cutting edge products that others have already made, providing that you do so smartly!

Unlimited Wealth

In order to understand that distribution can generate a fortune for you without your own personal investment in development or manufacturing, it is important to understand a key economic principle. Economist Paul Pilzer wrote about this principle at length in his work, "The New Wellness Revolution", where he called it the principle of "unlimited wealth".

Effectively, the concept is that we live in a society where people tend to find their passion and then make a career out of that passion. This works since we end up doing the same thing over and over to get perfection and amazing results. Over time, this increases the value and generates more return on investment.

However, there is one roadblock to this unlimited wealth – distribution.

The Secrets behind Distribution

Putting efforts into distribution is the key to ensure profitability yet revenue. While physical distribution is key to make profits through distribution, so is education the public about the demand and supply of the product in discussion.

As you well know, you may have access to the most innovative and valuable product ever seen in the Wellness industry, but unless you can communicate the need for that product to clients and consumers, you aren't going to be able to move a single unit.

Moreover, you do not need just great amount of attention for details but there is a need to demonstrate the value of the product to as many people as possible. This may seem to be a daunting task but once you get a hang of it, it's actually simple and easy as the task is repetitive. You need to take a look at the market condition and salvage it accordingly. Of course, there are few entrepreneurs who have made it big through development and manufacturing of core technology like Apple's Steve Jobs. However, a majority of people have done so not through developing and manufacturing the most innovative product, but through distributing these products to the end consumers.

Indeed, trends are moving in such a way as to favor distributers over manufacturers. To see the truth of this, one need only look at how physical retailers have changed over the last few decades. It used to be the case that the most successful retailers were specialty shops and department stores. However, that is now changing, such that the most successful physical retailers are "big box" mass merchandisers like Wal-Mart, Costco, and Target.

These companies do not have the same high quality of goods and services yet they continue to dominate the marketplace. This translates to the importance of distribution. Often, the product is secondary rather the distribution is primary. Today, a new genre of retail entity has emerged in the market place – mass merchandising in one category of goods.

For example, Lowe's is a category buster that focuses all of its efforts on distributing home repair and renovation supplies. Staples or Office Depot are category busters in the field of office supplies and paper goods. The lesson here is clear. If you don't have the resources to be a wide-scale mass merchandiser who provides competent and effective distribution of a whole category of Wellness-related goods, don't worry about it. Instead, simply focus on a single category of Wellness goods that you CAN effectively promote and distribute, and the results will be just as good. It's all about specialization. For example, say that you love to cook, so you know more about the availability of fine high-quality Wellness ingredients than anyone else involved in the Wellness industry at the moment.

Zero Marginal Production Costs

While passion plays a major part in effective marketing, and especially so in an industry like Wellness, it is unfortunately not the only consideration which a profitable distributer of goods must keep in mind. In addition to marketing what you know and love, you should also seek to move those items which you can make the most money on per unit.

Let us take an example. Supposedly, you are all about wellness foods. You are in a convention when you bump across a wellness-minded chef who supplies his own gourmet whole-grain ravioli made by finest and healthy ingredients. You discuss the matter with him and come to an agreement where you decide to distribute his goods locally through your own distribution pipeline as a re-seller. You will get a volume discount from the chef. Let us assume that you pay $2.00 for each product package and spend $3 on distribution costs. This way, you sell the product for $8 each. This is $3 profit for each of the package you sell.

What is Zija? What is in Zija? What is Moringa? 21

On the other hand, you meet another wellness-minded supplement manufacturer who creates a supplement, which is not readily available in the market yet the ingredients are available for you locally. You create the same reselling agreement with them. Due to the local availability of the ingredients, the cost to acquire the supplement will be $0.50 and it costs $2.0 to distribute. Since the ingredients are scarce elsewhere, you can charge a premium of $10 per package, which people are willing to pay. Your profit on each supplement will be $7.50, which is more than twice of the profit you'll make on ravioli.

Even though your passion is Wellness food and you're more personally interested in the ravioli than in the supplement, it only makes sense that you would place more emphasis on the supplement, due to the higher return on investment and profit potential.

Your mindset as an entrepreneur is based on a principle that has helped the other mass merchandisers to be successful. For some goods and products, the total cost of product for each unit can be reduced to virtually nothing. This is known as maximization of profits, in that the money you make from reselling such a product is pure profit since the sheer volume and economies of scale has reduced the cost to manufacture it to nothing.

By putting in enough time to research, you will find this is true for most of the products sold in the wellness industry. All you need to do is research and look around until you find products that have the unique characteristics to help you be successful yet distribute it for virtually zero cost.

Direct Marketing

Of course, it should also be mentioned that the price at which you can market goods is not determined entirely by circumstance or by the original developer or manufacturer. Indeed, there are certain things which a distributer can do to cut costs sharply, simply by modifying the method through which the product is distributed. Far and away, the most popular method for reducing costs, both for the distributer and consequently for the end user, is "direct marketing".

Direct marketing, in this sense, refers simply to the movement of products directly to the client through some interface, either person-to-person, or in more recent times, via a website, that is in some ways the opposite of simply stocking a store and letting clients come to you. There are many who chastise direct marketing for being "outdated" in this day and age when people are said to value speed and convenience over demonstrated value, but this is simply not true. In 2005, more than 100 billion dollars were raised through sales via direct marketing alone.

Direct Marketing agents find consumers, sign them up to orders and let the manufacture and the web fulfill them. This is social marketing and it is absolutely cutting edge.

Moreover, it is estimated that at least 75% of the United States population still engages in purchasing behaviors through the direct marketing or direct sales channel. So much for the idea that direct selling and marketing is dead.

When you opt for direct selling, you can take control of the costs of everything that you will sell. You may think strategically to ensure you have little overhead and that it costs you nothing to "stock" the merchandise. In such a case, the only cost will be the cost of item itself and the cost to distribute the product. There is nearly always something you can do to trim away at either of these and still turn a profit. This allows you to maximize the profit value of each item you sell through your direct sales approach.

Direct Selling and Residual Income

Another major benefit of direct marketing or direct sales is that it can bring you a good deal of residual income. It must be stated, for the record, that there are two key types of income with which you must be concerned if you really hope to make a fortune in any market, much less the Wellness market. Active income is income that you receive directly in response to some labor that you carry out.

For instance, if you mow someone's lawn as a kid, and receive $20 for the job, that's direct income. To get another $20, you're going to have to find another lawn to mow. Now let's say you grow up to be a famous rock musician (congratulations!). You write a hit song early in your career, and a month after the album comes out, you get a nice fat royalty check for thousands. That might be considered direct income as well. However, the next month you'll get another check for royalties on that album, assuming it continues to sell. If you've written a real hit, you may still be getting royalty checks years into the future.

Even if you never write another song besides that first hit, it can continue to generate income for you long past the initial effort you put into it. That is residual income, and how people truly get wealthy. Of course, it's not just for artists and rock musicians. You can earn residual income off of stock investments, books that you write, and, most importantly for you, Wellness goods that you sell through direct marketing!

How does this work? It's quite simple. Recall that we've established that distributing a product really consists of two actions: the first is the education of the client that the product exists and that it offers benefits to the client and the second is actually getting the product to them. The first can be difficult, but the second is nearly always a breeze. However, if you do a good job of direct marketing, you're not just moving product, but establishing long term relationships with clients that will continue to pay you dividends well into the future. If you sell a client a supplement that really addresses his or her needs and changes his or her life in a profound way, that client will almost certainly continue to buy that supplement through you, month after month. This means that, just like the rock star, you put in the initial effort to demonstrate the value of the product, and then it leads to long-term residual income that pays off well into the future.

Evaluating a Direct Marketing Opportunity

Having explored how direct selling can be valuable to a distributer working in the Wellness industry, it is important to cover a few logistical points. For instance, how do you know what products to work within your direct marketing venture? In order to make this determination, it's necessary to engage in a little psychological exercise. Basically, you'll need to place yourself in the position of the client and ask some fundamental questions about the value of what you're marketing —and most importantly, you'll have to answer truthfully.

For any given product that you have the opportunity to market, place yourself in the client's position and ask yourself if you had never heard of this product before now, would it be something that you would have an interest in buying? If you can't imagine yourself ever seeing the value in a product and wanting to buy it for your own use, you can't reasonably expect a client to see that value either. In short, if you wouldn't buy it, neither will the client. This means that, no matter how attractive a product might be in terms of price or cost, or no matter what sort of relationship you have with the manufacturer or developer, you should not attempt to sell it if it doesn't meet this "honest" evaluation. Otherwise, it will drag down your efforts to make your fortune in Wellness.

Another vital question to ask yourself, when determining whether or not you want to attempt to add a product to your direct marketing repertoire, is whether or not the product really contributes to Wellness.

While wellness is an emerging trend, there will be people who would treat it with respect while others who will claim it is a fad to earn a quick buck. But as someone who knows something about health and sickness, you know that Wellness is not a fad but a major trend, so if you offer a client a legitimate product they will become long term purchasers. It is an enduring principle of human physiology that is not going to change anytime soon.

Therefore, it is important for those who seek a fortune in the wellness industry to work with respect and integrity and sell products that are true and legitimate. This will help in longevity of your business and will also give you of satisfaction that you are truly contributing to the wellness industry. This is what generates the loyalty that produces lasting client and marketer relationships and, in turn, residual income from those same loyal clients who order month after month. If your product does not truly seem to contribute to long-term Wellness, it is not worth your time to sell it. Move on. It's also worth mentioning at this point that some direct marketers choose to work for a direct marketing organization, rather than pick and choose their own products from developers and vendors that they personally seek out. This can have its advantages and disadvantages. The primary advantage, of course, is that one has to put little effort into finding products and goods to take to the market; one simply offers what is available through the organization and collects the profits there from.

One may also have access to a wider variety of higher quality merchandise this way, depending on the organization for which one integrates with. However, there are some major disadvantages that you should look out for as well. For example, most of the organizations charge some sort of fee. This fee may be totally fair at times but at the other times it may be exorbitant and may mar the feasibility of executing your endeavor.

Sometimes these organizations can exhibit predatory behaviors that are not really in the best interests of direct marketers, but rather exist primarily to make a profit for the owners of the organization. In short, the quality of direct marketing organizations differs wildly, and if you're going to work for one, you had best be sure that it's a legitimate organization that offers what you're looking for before you cast your lot with them.

Luckily, there are some guidelines you can use to make such a decision. As Pilzer points out in his book, the Direct Sales Association offers a set of guidelines in the form of a "Code of Ethics" that all forthright marketing organizations should follow.

Before joining any organization, think about the following factors:

• Start-Up Costs

A high quality direct marketing organization will want to forge new relationships with marketers, and will thusly have few barriers to entry. The start-up costs associated with joining will generally be quite low. This is because well-established functional marketing organizations have the confidence that a marketer will be around for the long term and allow the company to profit that way. However, a fly by night organization that hopes to exploit marketers knows that marketers aren't going to stick around for long once they realize what's going on and consequently they want to charge as much as possible upfront so that they can make all the profit they can before the sellers run away. Consider high start-up costs a dire warning sign about the quality of any marketing organization.

• Options to Purchase

A high quality marketing organization will recognize that products sell differently in each region or that marketers will have unique specialties and be better able to move one type of product than another. As such, they are all too happy to let marketers pick and choose what products they wish to try and market, and allow sellers the option to purchase products or not purchase products. Again, they adopt the long-term view that allowing a marketer to grow his or her business organically is better for long-term profits than forcing them to adhere to some rigid guidelines that aren't going to work for everybody. If an organization requires you to sell certain products that you aren't sure about, think twice before venturing with them.

• Fees

The bottom line, in regards to fees, is that a high-quality direct marketing organization will only charge you money based on the products that you sell. The more products you sell, the more of a fee will go to the company, because they take a small percentage from each sale. This is a fair deal, and the way it should be, because it means that both the company and the marketer have an equal interest in getting products sold. Unscrupulous marketing organizations, however, generally require sellers to pay certain fees regardless of whether or not they actually sell anything. The problem with this is that the company has no incentive to actually help promote and facilitate sales. Once they hook the marketer, they're already making a profit off their fees, so they could care less whether the marketer is actually able to get the products to an end user or not. Inquire upfront about the nature and quantity of fees before joining any marketing organization.

• Return Policy

Lastly, a high-quality marketing organization will allow you to return unsold inventory after a period of time. Everyone makes mistakes in business, but they need not be catastrophic. Suppose that you overestimated the value of a particular product and ordered much more of it than you were able to move.

Moringa Oleifera – The Modern Ambrosia

What is Moringa?

Imagine a tree of life that will cure most common diseases, fulfills your nutritional needs, and helps you with a healthy transformation. Moringa, properly known as Moringa Oleifera, is a miracle tree loaded with three times more iron than spinach, tons of vitamins, and is a power source for antioxidants.

It is believed that Moringa is the most useful tree in the world. It is loaded with beta-carotene, Vitamin C, Vitamin C, Protein, Iron, and Potassium.

Fact or Fad?

You may be wondering why you have not heard about Moringa. One of the reasons for this is that the mainstream media does not feel the urgency to create awareness about an affordable yet natural source of fitness, energy, and well-being; they are still in favor of helping corporate sponsors in selling expensive, mass-produced products. However, Moringa Oleifera did manage to make it to specific media streams such as the Dr. Oz Show and the Discovery Channel. It has also been reviewed scientifically in science and medical journals, highlighted, and recognized on the web and in print.

Another reason why not everyone knows Moringa Oleifera is due to its varied names - clarifies tree, horseradish tree, mother's best friend, etc. A simple Google search for the following keywords can tell you more about the power of Moringa. The statistics are already out there.

- **moringa cancer**

- **moringa diabetes**

- **moringa detoxification**

- **moringa water**

I started using Zija when a close friend of mine introduced me to it! He asked me to trust him and I did and boy am I glad I did!! I lost 20 pounds the first month and I have now lost 50 pounds and feel better than I have in several years. My whole family is now taking Zija. Rob A. – Mayfield, KY

The benefits of Moringa

Moringa is a powerhouse of multi-vitamins. Effectively, Moringa is rich in Vitamin A, Vitamin B1, Vitamin B2, Vitamin B3, Vitamin C, Calcium, Chromium, Copper, Iron, Magnesium, Manganese, Phosphorous, Potassium, Protein, and Zinc. As well, and of interest to vegans, Moringa leaves contain all the essential amino acids (proteins) to build strong, healthy bodies.

Medicinal uses of Moringa Oleifera

The medicinal use of Moringa Oleifera goes back to Bible and even the Egyptian culture. It has been used as a preventative medicine for thyroid, stomach, kidney, and liver problems. Effectively, it is a complete nutritional supplement with more Vitamin A than carrots, more Vitamin C than oranges, and more calcium than milk. It has powerful antioxidant properties, great fighting tool against skin cancer, prevents cysts, tumors, and helps against prostrate growth.

Native medicine's wisdom states that Moringa Oleifera can be used for cancer treatment. It is also known to have antibody features since the late 1940's when an Indian research team found a compound in it called pterygospermin. Since a long time, Moringa Oleifera has been a big contributor in reducing diabetes, anemia, and high blood pressure. Moreover, its anti-inflammatory properties reduces pains, is effective against arthritis, joint pain, migraine, rheumatism, and headaches.

Moringa Oleifera purifies water

The extract of Moringa Oleifera is used to purify water as it removes solid particles and bacteria. It is also used to remove solids in drinking water. As a purifier, it removes any traces of aluminum contamination. In many cases Moringa can purify water within 1 hour:

Moringa Oleifera as a weight loss agent

Moringa Oleifera does magic for those looking to shed their weight as well. Essentially, it provides 42% of the recommended daily diet requirement for protein and calcium. Moringa leaves can be consumed raw, can be cooked, or taken as a tea. Preparing for a cup of tea? You may want to stop right there and consider Moringa Tea since it provides dieters with rich supplementary vitamins, minerals, and proteins, thus putting a stop to fats and high-calorie carbohydrates.[1] It is rich in important nutrients to nurture your body, make you feel fuller, and help you with your diet plan without compromising on your eating habits while supplementing your body to help build a strong immune and nervous system.

[1] Talalay Paul. 2008. A Nibble of Prevention. John Hopkin's Research

Moringa for Pregnant and Lactating Mother

Eating healthy food is of utmost importance for a pregnant and lactating mother. Our body needs protein, calcium, iron, and folic acid more than it does before pregnancy. However, healthy does not mean a mother-to-be start eating twice as much. It means that you need to choose food that is rich in nutrients for the baby. Balanced and sensible meals are the best for the mother and the baby.

Moringa Oleifera is proven to cure and prevent malnutrition in children, pregnant, and lactating mothers.[2] Moreover, Moringa leaves are proven to improve malnourished children in a matter of few days. Moringa and its products have been known to combat malnutrition especially among nursing mothers and infants. Moringa also increases the flow of production of breast milk. Simply put, if Moringa is provided as a source of nutrition for pregnant women, it can help in creating the ultimate breast milk, which will be instrumental in a healthy child.

So how do you grow this miracle tree? In the next chapter, we will discuss in details what it takes to cultivate Moringa and how to get the most out of it.

I have been an athlete my whole life; and needless to say, physical fitness and health are very important to me! Five years ago I married my high school sweetheart and in the past two years we have been blessed with two beautiful baby boys. I was unhappy with the fact that I had gained 60 lbs. with each pregnancy and no matter what I did, I could not get that last 20 lbs. of weight back off….. until I was introduced to Zija's weight management system!

In the first month of consistently taking Zija products, 15 pounds melted off, without exercise. I have lost an additional 7 pounds and am continuing to lose. Oh, and did I mention that I have a TON of energy now!

Lindsay H. Campbellsville, KY

[2] Fuglie Dr. Lowell. Church World Service nutrition program, West Africa - Dakar, Senegal.

Did you know:

Moringa has the highest protein ratio of any plant on earth1

Moringa is renowned throughout the world as an abundant source of nutrition by The National Geographic Society, The National Science Foundation, The United Nations World Food Program, and the National Institutes of Health.

"…perhaps like no other single species, this plant has the potential to help reverse multiple major environmental problems and provide for many unmet human needs."2

Natural Benefits from Moringa:

- Nourishes body's immune system

- Promotes health circulation
- Supports normal blood glucose levels
- Natural anti-aging benefits
- Anti-inflammatory support
- Promotes healthy digestion
- Heightens mental clarity
- Increases energy

Zija products are formulated for bioavailability and easy absorption in the body. Each Zija beverage contains a proprietary blend of organically harvested Moringa leaf, fruit, and seed.

1. "The Miracle Tree", Dr. Monica Marcu

2. "NIH Celebrates Earth Day 2008", NIH Record, Vol LX, No. 6, March 21, 2008

Cultivating Moringa

Cultivating Moringa is probably not as easy as growing carrots in your backyard. It is perhaps one of the most resilient plants. It is versatile; it can grow perhaps anywhere irrespective of the conditions: from India to Sri Lanka, Malaysia, Africa, Central and South America to the mighty Himalayas. Apparently, Moringa cultivation is one of the sources of bread and butter for Africa. It has said to address obesity, diabetes, blood pressure, hunger, etc. especially in the hungrier parts of the world.

Moringa tree can grow in semi-arid, tropical, and sub-tropical areas. Places such as South California and Florida are good places to grow it. During winters, cultivation of Moringa Oleifera needs to be taken to warm greenhouses since it can tolerate low temperatures but not as low as below freezing. While the best conditions for Moringa to grow are dry and sandy soil, it can also bear poor soil.

Moringa is a fast growing tree that can grow up to 3 meters just in the first year. It grows as tall as 10-12 meters, grows best in subtropical and tropical climates, bearing fruits continually. However, it grows best in dry and sandy soil. Ideally, semi-desert conditions make the best environment to cultivate Moringa since it provides both shade and food.

Here is how Moringa is cultivated:

1. **Find a sunny place**
2. **Make square holes in the ground 30-60cm deep**
3. **Fill in these holes with lose ground**
4. **Plant Moringa seeds 1cm deep**
5. **Water the ground but do not overdo it.**
6. **Within 1-2 weeks, Moringa leaves will sprout out of the ground.**

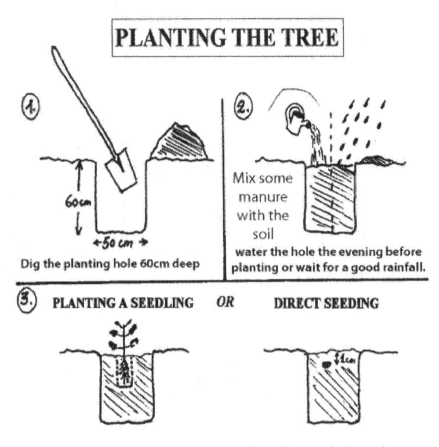

Sounds easy enough, right? Hold on your horses, as it is not that easy. To give you an idea, it's a lot of back breaking work!

What is Zija? What is in Zija? What is Moringa?

Moringa tree image supplied by Trees of the Future.

There are many factors critical to growth of Moringa. It may or may not grow in your backyard. Moreover, it requires utmost care, cultivation, and most importantly – time! If you are too busy, or live in a city, or in a country where this is not possible, a supplement is the next way. We'll get to this later.

At the outset of this book, we talked about Moringa and how it is being used as a means to make money. It is very prominent source of income in Africa. It came into limelight after it was discussed on the Dr. Oz Show. However, despite its many benefits it is still a niche product. That is where you can leverage it and make money since not everyone is aware of its benefits.

We will talk more about this in the next chapter.

Getting Started with Network Marketing Right – the Lifeblood of making Money

Why do you want to be successful? Why should you have this success that so few do? Why are you the one that people should search out for answers?

For some, it's easy to answer: "I want to be rich!" "I want to drive a fancy car and have a big house etc." "I have worked hard all my life and I deserve it!"

But the truth of the matter is this one question: why?

Why do you want to have that fancy car and big house? What's your reason? Why do you feel you deserve financial freedom? And most importantly, what are you willing to do to get them? If you aren't willing to do much, it's probably not going to happen.

"The definition of insanity is doing the same thing over and over again and expecting a different outcome." - Albert Einstein

This famous quote was applicable back when Big Al was around and guess what - some things don't change. The point is that what you've done up until now, as you're reading this book, has gotten you to this point in your life. That could be a great thing, but maybe not, who knows? You are the only one that can make that judgment. With this book and with the right direct marketing opportunity, you can get very far in life. But what's the answer? What's the trick and where do you start? Basically if you start with only one change, one little push to get you started, it would have to be this:

Get out of your comfort zone!

That's it, easy, simple, and to the point. According to Einstein and every other successful person past and present, you have got to get out and do something different if you want different results! This brings us back to the question of why?

Your why must be personal and unique to you, only you can choose it and it must be strong enough for you to be able to draw strength from it. It must be precise and specific. So the old, "I want to be rich because I want to buy lots of stuff and make my friends jealous," just doesn't fly anymore. To get specific results you must be specific in what your goals are.

Reflect back and think about your inspiration for everything you do in your life. That is your why! More specifically, the 'why' you want to be financially independent and have the freedom to be with your inspiration anytime you want to be.

Get a job!?

The 'why' is specific and will last the test of time. Of course the big house, fancy car and paying off the bills are desires as well but after that goal is achieved then what? Quit? Pack it up and get a J.O.B? (By the way job or J.O.B. stands for "Just over Broke"). Your "why" must be something lasting, an ongoing goal.

Ask yourself now what is your why? Be specific. A great trick is to write your goal on a piece of paper and keep it in your pocket, and when things become discouraging, because they do occasionally for everybody, take it out and read it aloud to yourself in the mirror.

Remember the only person that can tell you that you can't is you! Nobody else has that power over you unless you give them that power! Even if you are quiet, shy or anti-social, your "why" must be strong enough to bust you out of that rut, 100% of the time, 99% isn't enough! Take some time and really figure out your reason for doing this, if it's not worthy then you will have an extremely hard time getting into that 5% success area or that top 1% that achieves financial freedom.

On June 5th, 2010, I was 236 lbs., wore a XXL shirt and a 42-inch pant. I was taking blood pressure and cholesterol medicines, suffered from headaches, arthritis, and numbness in my face. Today Sept. 7th I weigh 186 lbs. I wear a size large shirt and a 36 inch pant. I no longer take blood pressure or cholesterol medicines. When I went to the doctor for a checkup, she asked if I was still taking my meds. I told her no, and she looked surprised.

I told her I was taking Zija. She took my blood pressure and it was 112 over 70. She said whatever you are doing keep doing it. I quit my meds "cold turkey" but I do not recommend anyone doing that. I was skeptical about this when I started but let me tell you Zija has changed my life! I feel better than I have in years. I do not sit in front of the TV anymore.

Dwayne H. – Mayfield, KY

"The most common way people give up their power is by thinking they don't have any." - Alice Walker

How do the rich get and stay rich?

Imagine a hypothetical situation where you are invited to dinner by a colleague because she knows you are new in town. You have very few friends at the time but this dinner party was hosted by a really nice old man. You enter the party and apparently you are the guest of honor; had you've known, you might have dressed up in something other than an old Mexico soccer jersey and shorts. Now you are immediately asked to sit with the host of the party and offered a glass of wine.

The host is an older gentleman perhaps in his mid 60's or so. He is extremely happy and wears a big smile throughout the whole evening. After a few glasses of wine he invites you into his office to show you his pride and joy, his book collection. You stand up and start to walk towards his office and when you look back to see where he was, you realize that he is in a wheelchair and he is a little slow at wheeling to his office, must have been the wine. Anyways after showing you his extensive collection of which you have no interest in, you ask him what the secret of his success is. He is wealthy and very happy despite being in a wheelchair. He replies with something that may leave an impression on many.

"Never stop learning..." he says "and you will always be happy and find a way to get what you desire." You are kind of shocked at his response being so simple but effective. It doesn't matter what happens in life as long as you keep on learning and improving yourself. If you do this one simple thing, you will always be happy. Teach yourself to be successful and you will be.

"Self-Education is the game Changer"

The point of this virtual experience was to help you understand a simple thing. You must continually keep improving yourself daily and constantly in order to keep bettering yourself as a leader. You must lead by example in order to keep others following you until they know what you know. At this point they will be wise enough to do the same with their own team and so on. But what do you do if you don't know anything? You must surround yourself with people that know more than you.

Anybody or anything can be inspiring and you can always keep learning if you open your mind and really read between the lines. A quick example of finding inspiration is movies. Movies are great way to relax. Use them as mini vacations whenever you can.

What is Zija? What is in Zija? What is Moringa? 43

Movies can be simple and fun and that doesn't only mean watching educational flicks, any movie will do! Read between the lines a little and you will be able to spot inspiration almost anywhere.

The first example is the movie "Troy" with Brad Pitt. He plays the role of Achilles, a warrior who the King of Greece is trying to "recruit" because he knows that Achilles is the best at what he does, nice strategy, sound familiar? Anyways Achilles wouldn't work with King because of the King's arrogance and selfishness. Knowing this, the King sends a lesser King, a friend of Achilles, to convince him to go to war supporting Greece. Achilles is young and brave, and he asks the lesser King how he could be "enthralled to such a pig of a king" and why would he follow someone like the King of Greece. The reply is what really stuck with me, the lesser King replied, "sometimes you have to follow in order to lead." So really what you learn here is that a true leader not only knows when it's time to step up and lead but also when it's time to step back and follow.

Inspirational quotes don't have to be quite as deep as the previous example; they can be simple, to the point and don't need to be made by a King. The next example comes from the movie "Sin City". In this movie, a street thug by the name of Marv, played by Mickey Rourke, is in the process of investigating a conspiracy murder and what he says about finding information was short simple and effective. He said, "When I need to find something out, I just go out and look for someone that knows more than me and I go and I ask them."

So as you can plainly see inspiration is in the eyes of the beholder. You can literally find it anywhere. Now think about "Scarface" and visualize the essence of the movie – he gets everything he desires. He looks up at the sky and in one of the only scenes where "Tony Montana" is calm and peaceful is when he sees an advert on a blimp passing by.

"The World is yours..." This is one of the most famous lines in the movie and also one of the most inspirational. It is important to try surrounding yourself with leaders that are better than you and what that does is it makes me a better leader. It's simple find somebody in your organization up the line somewhere that can help you learn what you need to know so you can be mentored into being the kind of person that this man or woman is.

There are many "gurus" out there that are full of themselves, but there are also many who have courses that are short, concise, to the point and will change your life. It is recommended to read as many books as you can and even if you only pick up a few things to add to your arsenal, after reading a whole bunch of them you will have your own library of amazing information and you will be able to approach any situation or person with confidence. Or better yet here's a list of must reads right now, books that every network marketer must have in their collection: "Rich Dad, Poor Dad" by Robert Kiyosaki, "The Compound Effect" by Darren Hardy, "The 45 second presentation" by Don Failla, "How to get Filthy Stinking Rich with Network Marketing" by Mark Yarnell, Valerie Bates, Derek Hall and Shelby Hall "Why We Want you to be Rich" by Donald Trump, and Robert Kiyosaki.

While we are on the subject of books, I want to tell you a story. During my research of this book, I ran across a retired speech writer who was working on another book on a network marketing company. We compared notes, and one thing that stood out for him, was a how many people found telephone calls for both prospecting and follow up/closing difficult. They had a hard time controlling the conversation, and one team had hired a network marketing telephone coach to teach them the art.

It all came down to keeping control of the phone call, and there was this handwritten file of things to say to keep or take back control. He said that small handwritten file contained 'lines' or single sentences that could be used in nearly any prospecting or closing call. They had proven themselves to be worth millions. Now, at the urging of many people, this coach turned them into a small Kindle book, and sells if for only .99, less than a dollar! 'If I can't sell it for its true value, millions of dollars, I'll sell it for a buck!'. This name is Dave Williams and this is the million dollar book:

US Amazon http://www.amazon.com/Simplest-Shortest-Powerful-Marketing-ebook/dp/B00BW7KJ38

Canadian Amazon http://www.amazon.ca/Simplest-Shortest-Powerful-Marketing-ebook/dp/B00BW7KJ38

UK Amazon http://www.amazon.co.uk/Simplest-Shortest-Powerful-Marketing-ebook/dp/B00BW7KJ38

Or just search Amazon for:

The Simplest, Shortest, Most Powerful MLM and Network Marketing Prospect Control and Closing Lines and Scripts

Where can I find info on what to say to people?

We often define leadership but it is important to understand that if you establish yourself as a credible leader, then people will follow you. This can be called as "the Alpha syndrome." It can also be called attraction marketing, the law of attraction, and many other things. We popularly call it Attraction Marketing They are all based around the fact that attraction is not a choice and understanding that is half the battle.

Let's try an example here. Choose your favorite celebrity, rock star, athlete, or motivational speaker; do you think that these people need to go door to door selling vacuum cleaners when they need to start building teams for their businesses? Of course not! Although if they did, now be honest, would you buy one? Chances are, yes, you would! Of course you would! To anybody who is reading this right now saying, "No I wouldn't!" here's an example.

Who's your idol?

Here's an example, you are a 9 to 5 office worker. Now you are at home relaxing, watching a movie online or a big sporting event, now your doorbell rings and its _____ (fill in the blank with your favorite singer, actor or athlete); supposedly, your favorite boxer is Evander Holyfield. So you answer the door and big Evander is standing there and he asks how you are and if you have a minute to watch a demonstration of his new super powered vacuum machine. You are in awe and you let him in.

He gives a quick demonstration of why his vacuum is the best and why joining his vacuum sales team is easy to join and that he would personally mentor you and help you become a killer vacuum salesman or women! How long would it take you to think about joining his team? Probably not long. Would you start grilling the "Real Deal Holyfield" about the specs on the vacuum? Of course not! Would you join? Yes, you probably would, why? Because that's the best vacuum machine you've ever seen? Not necessarily! The vacuum cleaner, although it is somewhat important, is not the main point. You would join just so you can be mentored by "the Real Deal". So you agree and he leaves.

What would you do? Sit back down and watch the end of the football match? No, of course not! You would most likely call your best friend and tell him the news. Would you say, "Guess what I'm a vacuum salesman now I'm so excited"? No, you would say something along the lines of, "Dude! Guess who just left my house? Evander Holyfield! Yeah man, I joined his biz and he's gonna be personally training me! Sweet eh?"…

By the way, Holyfield take Zija products!

Now you see the power of Attraction Marketing. You can use anybody in the previous example, Donald Trump, Robert Kyosaki, Beyoncé, Will Smith or whoever you want and chances are that you and everybody you know would grab the opportunity. Why? The reason is that we, the people, are hard wired to follow leaders,

What is Zija? What is in Zija? What is Moringa? 47

it's an animal instinct that can be called "the Alpha syndrome." Wolf packs follow the strongest wolf and trust him to lead the pack at all costs for two reasons:

1) He is the strongest and nobody can oppose him

2) Because it's easier to follow the leader and get in tight with the top dog, (pun intended) than it is to lead yourself.

Within my first week I lost 4 pounds. Every week afterwards, I noticed that I was losing more and more. Finally, after the 4th week, I weighed myself and I had lost a total of 20 pounds!! I cried for over an hour!! With such an emotional change, I kept up the system. I was finally a believer!!I have been doing the Zija Weight Management System for 7 weeks as of April 30th.

I have lost a total of 32 pounds. I have become beyond emotional with my weight loss! I cry every time I buy new clothes, I am so excited!! I haven't been this size in over 5 years. Zija has changed my life in way that I cannot even begin to imagine.

Jessica R., KY

Lions are the same, actually most animals are the same. Suppose you live in a remote location and love it there. However one thing that you're not fond of, being a dog lover is that there are many stray dogs. But, even they can serve as the perfect example, how long will a stray dog last alone on the streets? Probably not long, but as soon as it joins a pack, its chances for survival increase. Of course there is a tussle here and there but you get my point, it's the basic need.

Nowadays it's the same as the top dog example. But the top dog doesn't have to be a male nowadays. Alpha Male? Doesn't have to be anymore. Oh, don't think so? One word, Oprah! No response? Exactly - Oprah is one of the most successful people in the world and she is living proof that an alpha doesn't have to be a male.

"I will just create, and if it works, it works, and if it doesn't, I'll create something else. I don't have any limitations on what I think I could do or be." - Oprah Winfrey

How to recognize the right people? "In a deck of cards there are only four aces." – Anonymous

In this business you must eventually build a team and this team that you build will strongly influence the outcome of your success. If you build a team of lazy, shy, or casual people, your income will be lazy, shy and casual. However if you build a team of explosive, motivated, optimistic people then your income will be explosive, motivated and optimistic. Catch the drift?

"I recruit people that my business needs, not that need my biz. That's helped me explode my business." – Anonymous

People that are successful in life have a better chance of being successful in Network Marketing or Direct Marketing. So you must find people that are successful in life if you want to be successful yourself one day. So what you need to do to begin with a list of people.

Let's go through a brief process here. Start with a top 25 list; we'll call this your warm market. Brainstorm a list of friends and family without making any quick judgments such as, "well maybe he will laugh at me or maybe he's not into this kind of thing," etc. Make your list and then put the names though a simple test.

Since taking this product I have noticed an increase in energy levels for myself as well as decreased joint and muscle pain. My wife as I mentioned is a physical therapist and she trains quite heavily, she enjoys all of the benefits that I mentioned above also. The testimony that I am most proud of is the fact that my Mother and my Father are both off of their blood pressure and their cho-

lesterol medication for the first time in 10 years as a result of drinking this beverage." Rodney A., - Hodgenville, KY

1. Are they optimistic or pessimistic?

2. Do they have any credibility or influence in their communities?

3. Are they coachable?

4. I would like to work with this person because…

Great, that's the simple version, here's the explanation of each:

1. Optimism vs. Pessimism

Optimistic people are open-minded and happy to learn new things. They are excited about life and their passion for life shows. They are always positive, (though nobody's perfect), and more often than not this person is quite happy about life. Pessimists are the opposite.

There is always something to complain about and they want to let you know that they are unhappy whether it be, "I'm always sick", or, "I don't have enough money", or even, "The weather is horrible here I can't do anything". The famous old quote that comes to mind is, "If life gives you lemons, make lemonade." Now we can add to that quote, if you don't know how to make lemonade find someone who does, ask them to teach you and then do it.

2. Is this person credible or do they have any influence in their community?

"Every sparrow knows an Eagle and every minnow knows a whale" – Valerie Bates.

This person, are they connected? Do they have any friends that are connected? What about their job, do they have a position of power? If yes, then this person is a perfect candidate for Network Marketing because this person has developed a following in his or her own circle of friends. This person is well respected and has influence. Let me say that again INFLUENCE is huge in this game. Salesmen are not necessary, but teachers, trainers, coaches, and others do very well in this business. No sales experience? Doesn't matter, nobody wants to be sold! But with that being said, people love to buy. Find people that will uphold the reputation of the opportunity to the standard that you will. In short, don't recruit the obnoxious town drunk!

My goal was to regain some energy and be healthier. After six weeks of the drink my cholesterol went from 263 to 146. My doctor was amazed and so was I. My husband lost 2 inches in his waist after just six weeks. We both have more energy. Debbie F., – Lexington, KY

3. Are they coachable?

Coachability is huge in this business! This fact cannot be overstated. You could be the most successful person in the world and you might be able to do extremely well, but if you aren't willing to learn, then you will not get anywhere.

Let's use an example. Let us suppose, you own a Mexican restaurant called Eddy's Shack. You have created this business from scratch, you started with a small stand for one year, and then expanded to a small restaurant and now it's a great medium size restaurant in a beautiful upper class area in the heart of the city. It's quite popular now after five years, and your cooking skills have grown along the way. So the point is that you can make Mexican food quite well thanks to mom and grandmas recipes and you are very happy about that. However, if you ever went to work at a Sushi restaurant, how many of your tortilla and enchilada making skills would transfer over? Not many, if any. So you would need to learn a new style of cooking, and you would be happy to do it.

What is Zija? What is in Zija? What is Moringa?   51

Now, on the other hand you have people that come to your restaurant to apply for work, some of them seasoned chefs, that have come to work for you and each from many different styles of cooking.

However, none of them have been Mexican food cooks so you have to flat out tell them that their previous Japanese and Chinese cooking experience, although it's quite exceptional, really is irrelevant in your Mexican kitchen where you make tortillas from scratch and Huaraches by hand. The difference is that some people are alright with that, and some people aren't.

Those that are willing to learn and are coachable are the ones you want to hire so you can teach them Mexican cooking.

Are you coachable?

In week one I was losing a pound a day. In the weeks and months to follow I have lost 32 pounds and am now 200 for the first time in 20 years. My energy levels are back to my college days and I no longer need my Coffee.

Eric L. – Dallas, GA

4. This one is fun because with this one you can build a hypothetical Dream team. I would love to work with this person because...

Perhaps he/she is well connected and would really excel at this type of business. Perhaps this is a person of influence and can really help to build this team with you. This person is fun to be around and always excited and optimistic. This person is a successful businessperson and people are drawn to him/her (attraction). This person is already a network marketer but his/her company has provided little to no training for this person and little to no support so this person is kind of stuck with his her company.

After ONE MONTH on Zija, had my blood work done for my 6 month checkup. Results? Triglycerides DOWN 40 points. Fasting blood sugar level down to 101, from 121. Overall cholesterol down 10 points with the GOOD cholesterol up a point. Sue C.

Entrepreneurs or people with that entrepreneurial spirit, these people are always searching for ways to better themselves and better their situation. This list is endless and you can fill in your own blanks….

Another key to sponsoring people is what NOT to do. You will see it happen 95% of the time with new people. The first thing they do is tell prospects about how their company is the best and it's going to be the next billion dollar company and that it's got the best stuff. It, It, It! It's all about the company…

Hard fact to understand is this: When a person joins or is thinking about joining your organization, they are doing it because of you!

There is something about you that strikes their fancy and they believe in you and what you are offering! Did you hear the keyword? YOU, YOU, YOU!

Tip: If you don't think you have the credibility to use YOU as the selling point, go up the line till you find somebody who does have the credibility.

Another horrible thing that maybe only happens in Asia is marketing people standing outside of malls and shopping centers and basically chasing down passing customers trying to recruit them into their opportunity. A lot of them will CHASE people trying to get them to fill out forms about products etc. It's quite a crazy thing to watch, one of these days you can go down there to a spot that you know and record for a while to get this point across.

"Don't chase people. Be yourself, do your own thing and work hard. The right people – the ones who really belong in your life - will come to you and stay." -Will Smith

Dr. Bowers got involved with Zija after 'seeing all the research', 'over 1400 different verified, proven, published articles' proving Zija and Moringa was a powerful health product. So he 'added Zija into his patient protocols' and 'monitored 30 patients on this product and only then', did he tried it himself. Now, '1600 hundred patients later…Moringa is the base he uses in his practice'. It 'helps get patients well, and results in health'.

Is Social Media worth all the hype?

What is Social Media? Well, what isn't it? Have you ever heard of a little thing called Facebook? Or perhaps Twitter? There are many more, Flicker, Pinterest and especially personal blogs. Which of these should you use? As many of them as you can possibly handle! The more, the better, seriously! There are many people who are flat out Facebook users and don't use anything else, or bloggers or tweeters. Also there may be people who switched over from Facebook to Google Plus because they got tired of "Facebook upgrades".

Nonetheless Facebook is a giant, a preferred platform and probably the most popular platform. But, why use all of them? Because some people only use Facebook, some only Twitter, and some only Google plus. Using only one is like going to a party and meeting five different people that could explode your business and only talking to one or two of them.

My Cholesterol was 199. It is steady at 145 now with ZIJA. Carolyn B., - Fort Meyers, FL

TALK ABOUT COMFORT ZONE!

So if you only focus on one then you are only concentrating on only one piece of the pie instead of all of it. You can use these social media platforms not only to keep in touch with your friends and family but also to spread the word for your business. Facebook has a huge number of daily users, and there are new accounts made every day!

In a nutshell

So the point is that Social Media never sleeps even though you must! Use Social media and take advantage of it! Social media is a must if you want to spread your message fast! So if you don't have a Facebook account, it's time to create one, it's free and it will help a lot.

TIP: Use Social Media to promote your opportunity!

After being forced out of a 13 yr. career in the U.S. Marine Corps due to medical problems, I had gained some weight and my medical problems worsened. I had a degenerative disc; a disc removed from my neck, a shoulder impingement, arthritic knees, a hip impingement, and surgically repaired hand. The aches and pains were unbearable and I had no energy. After consuming Zija I noticed considerable improvements. Less aches and pains, more energy, and I was losing weight. Joel E., – Bowling Green, KY

Super-Secret Tip: Outsource your Social Media campaign.
What is outsourcing?

Outsourcing is another major trend you should be aware of and be using as much as possible. There is a rule in Direct Marketing called the 80/20 rule. It says, among other things, you should spend 80% of your time prospecting and recruiting, and 20% (or less) doing admin type work. This is where outsourcing comes in.

You need to outsource as much of the dull, boring, repetitive work as you can, so you can focus on what you like to do, and what earns you money. Activity vs. Productivity. If you focus on productivity you will be earning, the more you outsource the more time you have for income producing activities. Your social media presence is a great credibility activity, good for '3rd party verification' and long term prospecting. Once it's up and working for you, delivering you prospects, you can focus in it and keep your outsourcers active building up 'internet mouse traps' – lead generators – in less well known social media sites and tools.

A great place to explore is Fiverr.com. It's a great beginning site for learning and using outsourcers. An outsourcer is a 'gun for hire'. It could be a copy-writer, graphic artist, music writer, singer, accountant, video maker, voice over artist, or social media administrator, you name it. There are even people who will create a Facebook page for you, or Twitter account, etc., and even run a social media campaigns for you. Each job on Fiverr.com is $5.00. If you search out 'social media campaign' on Fiverr, you'll find many outsourcers willing to run this type of campaign for $5 per week.

Even if you know how to do this, you are better off outsourcing it. Once you are earning more money, move up to a better outsourcer. Take a look at Elance.com, Freelancer.com, Odesk, etc. You can find many on Google if you search outsourcer sites, or freelance sites.

The major point here is if you don't want to do the social media work, get out outsourced. It is manageable and it is affordable. You can't afford NOT to do it.

Dr. Hadryan Vaughn surgeon in Montgomery, Al, "I tried the product' and noticed 'energy, clarity…everything fell in line'. He shared it with is mother, a cancer survivor and noticed his father was taking it too. He 'did a lot of research on the product, and decided to share it with his patients'.

What kind of business is best for you?

My name is Dr. Johnnie Green and my background is in Chiropractic. As a former collegiate athlete, I participated in every event from the 400 meter dash to the 10,000 meter run as well as some field events. Although, I was able to have a successful 4 year track & field career, I suffered from 5 stress fractures during that time frame and pain had become a norm. The results--I had severe tendonitis after graduation.

After taking two cans of the product per day for 4 days, the tendonitis had diminished. In addition to that, before I only ate breakfast about twice a week, and I was never a "morning person." Although, breakfast is the most important meal of the day, I was constantly missing out and my energy levels were always down. However, I have witnessed a significant increase in my energy levels, and I am now more focus than ever. I am sleeping better at night, my metabolism has altered, and my diet is so much healthier. -Dr. Johnnie G., Beattyville, KY

Once again we will take a hypothetical example for this section. You can use these examples when talking to prospects, by explaining what you are about to read, to your prospect, you'll close them on networking:

Let's frame this as: Online Business vs. Brick and Mortar Business

As we have discussed in our earlier examples, we are assuming that you are a business owner and you own both, a restaurant and a Network Marketing company distributorship. Both have their advantages and both have their disadvantages.

Restaurant (Your brick and mortar business)

First off with a restaurant you must find a location. The old adage "Location, Location, Location" immediately comes to mind. Although it's true, it's not entirely that easy. Prime locations are very expensive because obviously they are in prime spots and the landlord knows that, so you're not going to get a lease for a low price.

Next you need to decide what to serve in that restaurant, in this case you serve Mexican food because you are a Mexican and you cook a lot of Mexican food. Another reason is that the Mexican Food in your location is well …. Let's just say it is not great. You feel good Mexican food is a needed in your area, and you can provide it. With you cooking and training people it saves you hiring a head Chef, however it requires a ton of your time.

Staff – Staff is probably the most difficult part of the whole equation. Robert Kiyosaki said it best in one of his books, "Workers work hard enough not to be fired…" It seems to be true in almost any industry.

The restaurant business is no different unfortunately. People in your restaurant start at the bottom and they work their way up, and earn more as they do. You usually find one of two things happens, if you are really strict, people tend to think of you as arrogant but at least they do what they are told. If you are really cool and buddy with them, they tend to slack off thinking "Ah, he's cool; he isn't going to say anything." Let's not get started on staff wages and benefits employee taxes and contributions, insurance, and more or we might be here all day.

Food Cost – This is self-explanatory but the thing about food is that it doesn't last forever and it goes bad pretty quickly, so if it's a slow week too bad. A lot of waste. The best part of restaurant business is you get to meet new people. Everybody's got to eat whether they are a Prince or a Pauper. That makes for a great mix of people that you get to meet. It is great for networking, and you can make some lifelong best friends.

What is Zija? What is in Zija? What is Moringa? 59

While owning a restaurant is might be profitable, it will be extremely time consuming and exhausting.

Multi-Level marketing company / Network Marketing Company

Great companies - There are many great companies out there with great products. It's common knowledge, or it should be, that network marketing company products are very high quality because you get what you pay for without the necessity of a middle man.

I began drinking Zija in Sep. of 2008. Because of it I no longer take pain meds and I have had 2 knee operations, bulging disc in my neck and just general wear and tear on my body. My whole being is so much better not just physically but emotionally as well. This is one product I will use the rest of my life. The skin care line has also had a big impact on my face, I can see the years of abuse slowly being reversed. Feeling great and looking great. Verda H., – Hodgenville, KY

Low cost of entry – This is the amount of money that you need to invest to get started, it ranges from company to company but usually you get started with as little as a few hundred dollars. No need for a location – gone are the days of having to fill your garage with cosmetics and powders just to become active in your company. Most companies encourage you to do everything online and some even go as far as setting up a web based store for each of its distributers. This way people can shop from their home and you can manage your business from anywhere you want as long as you have a web connection. Truly a business never affected by the weather.

Staff – In most network marketing companies, you are encouraged to recruit (sponsor); however, you can approach and recruit whom you please. You don't have to work with that guy who is always talking wasting your time at water cooler nor must you endure an employer breathing down your neck. You can build a team that YOU want to work with.

Dr. Tiffany Crutcher Montgomery, Al, The 'product simply works', after 'four days her mother can walk without pain'. Dr. Crutcher says nurses, doctors and medical professionals are the best recruits.

Low maintenance cost – Most companies have a minimum requirement for you to purchase monthly called the "autoship". Autoship lets you "set and forget" that you need to purchase this small amount of product for personal usage. It is recommended that you use the products that you offer because if you don't think that they are worth using, nobody else will.

An autoship order means you commit to a small monthly purchase. Some negative people will see this as a turn off, but consider the view from optimistic people: If you had a downline organization of over 1000 people, wouldn't you want them to be committed to a monthly autoship plan? People will do what you do, so get on the plan for your chosen company from day one, so you can tell that same story once over and over.

"Never Again" - One problem with network marketing is that it has such a bad reputation due to horrible independent distributers from all different companies' pressure selling and lying to get ahead in their companies compensation systems. Most people have been or know somebody that has been burned by an 'old school' MLM Company and they vowed "never again," so it's a tough sell.

"Pyramid Scheme" - People are really freaked out by pyramid games, which are illegal so it is best to know your pay plan and be able to ward off any fear that the prospect might initially feel.

Pressure Tactics - People love to buy but hate being sold – pretty self-explanatory but people love to shop and spend their heard earned dough on goodies that they want but they hate the feeling

What is Zija? What is in Zija? What is Moringa?   61

when a fast talking salesman tries to sell them on something they don't feel they need.

So, share, don't sell. If you are a super slick sales type, you will find it does not work in network marketing, because your prospects are going to notice that they could not do what you do.

Bottom line: Network marketing is not perfect, it requires a person to get out of their comfort zone, but at the same time, so does running any business. The risk vs. reward factor however is heavily sided on the network marketing business vs. a traditional one.

Which is better?

There is of course no simple answer; it's all about point of view. What came first the chicken or the egg? What color is better, red or blue? What food tastes better, Japanese or Indian? These can all be answered with your own opinion. Bottom line is to educate yourself, to do your due diligence and to open your mind to opportunities that are all around you. One last thing on this topic, network marketing has and will continue to create multiple multimillionaires from now till forever, just depends on what you are willing to do for it!

Which MLM company is the best for you?

Some of you may already have an MLM company that you are with, that is fine and some of you are using this book as a baseline that's fine too. Some of you may not even have an MLM company, that's great. I encourage you to read this chapter over and over as many times as you need to for it to really sink in.

Dr. Fred Valdes, (MD). Dr. Valdes read the overwhelming evidence on the product research, then he decided to try the products himself. Very soon, his cholesterol went down, he lost 28 pounds, and more. He now offers Zija to everyone.

The 3 T's of Success

The three T's is a philosophy that has been developed to determine what a successful MLM company must have in order for you to succeed. If even just one of these T's is missing, it is probably not going to work; it is still possible but not probable.

Trust: The first T is trust. This means that your products, whatever they are, must work. Therefore, you must believe in them so people can trust and believe in you when you are talking to them about these products.

Let us take another hypothetical situation. Let us suppose Andy is in a college and he is already aware of the fact of network marketing and the power that it had. Actually, he had just dropped out of college, he was home, and he came across this flash presentation and this website about this new company. They had a beautiful flash presentation and man he was excited. He did a little research and although the internet was not very developed in those days, he had found somewhere that this product would pretty much cure MS, Multiple sclerosis. Now he didn't know much about MS, but it turns out that he had a soccer friend whose mother had a pretty extreme case of MS. So he thought wow if it could help her it would be amazing because he knew she was suffering.

Also he thought that 'wow'; here would be the first success story for this new product. So, to make a long story short, he made an appointment with this lady and she basically told him about what MS was and it was rough. He explained to her that he had found this new product that was unknown and that it may and most likely would help her. She agreed to try it.

Now, sadly, this product didn't do a thing to help her. This lady trusted him and but product did nothing and although she probably doesn't even remember years later, it still bothers Andy. He tried to sell it for a month or so after hearing that the product did not help the woman, but he could not do it. This lady is still fighting MS today.

There is an old rule of life: No one will love you more than you love yourself. The same is true about trust.

No one will trust you more than you trust yourself. For people to trust you, you must trust yourself and believe yourself. Your product must work so that you will sound credible and then you will develop a relationship with your customers. Once you have an unshakable belief, you will go to the top.

Does that mean you have to have dramatic results with your product? No, but it helps. However, if you meet and talk with a large number of people who have had dramatically positive result from a product, that should help you build your own unshakable belief. If your product concerns helping children learn to read, and you have no children, does mean you can't develop as strong a unshakable belief as the parents of one? No, only a fool says 'I can't sell something that does do anything for me, even if it helps others'. That kind of attitude is the same as suggesting a person confined to a wheel-chair cannot sell running shoes. That kind of thinking does not belong in this century. It's called 'stinkin' thinkin''.

Training: The next T is training. Training from your company is super important. If they don't teach you how, then how can you possibly learn what to do? A system that is easy to use, like training videos and manuals, PowerPoint presentations etc. are necessary if the company, and you, are to be successful. However even more important that the training provided by the company, is your team and upline support. They must be knowledgeable and must be willing to help you and they must be aware of how they got to where they are. Dependable, friendly and humble. This is critical if you are to be successful in this company.

What is Zija? What is in Zija? What is Moringa? 65

There is a much bigger reason for this then just for you to learn what to do. Much bigger. What if you did come to the table knowing what to do? But you had no one else in your company or in your upline team that did. What's the problem? The problem is you would be forced to spend lots of YOUR time training all of your new people. No one would want to be trained by anyone else, since you were so good.

I started drinking Zija in December of 2008. I had scoliosis as a child and developed arthritis and fibromyalgia. Within 2 months my pain was gone and also the swelling in my left knee. I was told my husband would be in a wheelchair by December 2009, he is still going, still walking. We know Zija is keeping him pain free and on his feet. Sue U. – Canmer, KY

You see, having training in place is not just a benefit to you now, it's a benefit to you as you build your team, so your new recruits are learning from the 'system' and not taking your time. Remember the 80-20 rule. If you are training new people, you are not recruiting. You want a company that offers a 'training system' that you can plug people into.

With technology nowadays you can communicate with somebody in Antarctica to someone in the North Pole, all you need is an internet connection. Your upline must be willing to coach and help you with whatever you need. Out of time is not an option however, it is recommended that you too schedule appointments at your upline(s) convenience because you are not likely the only person that they are helping. Let us take another hypothetical situation. Let us suppose you have an upline member of your team in the US, Alan Murray. He is a world bench press record holder and when you were interviewing him, he never mentioned this once.

Everybody else you talk to about him mentions this great achievement about him, but he himself never did, humble… Now let us take another situation. Suppose you joined a MLM company, a few months back. This company had a decent product; the energy product was based off the Acai Brazilian berry, which is a nutritious plant. Therefore, it passed the product test and the potential was definitely there so you jumped in. Your sponsor this time was the wife of one of your best friends, she was pretty much guaranteeing you that you wouldn't have to do anything except autoship, and you would get rich. Sounded like a pretty good deal and you were always looking for that opportunity. Again, to cut a long story short, you put in zero effort, zero time, and zero promotion. So can you guess how much money you made? Yes, that's right - ZERO, ha!

Gabe has had Juvenile Rheumatoid Arthritis since he was 5 years old. Since taking Zija, Gabe has had a miraculous turnaround. He has been able to remove his orthotic insoles from his shoes as well as his ankle braces. His pain level has decreased to almost zero. We are true believers in the benefits of Zija. It has improved Gabe's quality of life tremendously!" Kellie S. - Hodgenville, KY

Well, there is no free lunch?

Timing: The third and final T is Timing! Think of some of those big well-known companies that have been around for 30 years or more, wouldn't you have loved to get in the ground floor on one of those 30 years ago? Of course, you would have, why? Because, if you got in at the beginning and after building an initial team that spread out, you would not have to lift a finger for the rest of your life.

Timing is undeniably the single most important thing in this business. If you know about something and YOU are the person to present this opportunity to the masses before they have even heard of it, how valuable is that? It is huge!

Sure, you could join another big company that is a household name and you might make some money but if you put in the same amount of time and the same amount of dedication in a company positioned for growth, you will be paid off a hundred-fold maybe even a thousand fold.

"Most new Network Marketing companies fail within the first 18 months" - Jessica Phillips

What this statement means is that if you get into a company too early it could also backfire. The company could go bankrupt before it takes off. Anybody who knows anything about business knows that it takes money to make money (at least for network marketing corporations that's true) and every company starts off in the hole and if it never takes off, it may never get out of the hole and just kind of implode instead of explode.

The reason is rapid growth. Once a company starts growing rapidly, the demand for product increases. Most new companies can't keep their manufacturing, raw material purchase fast enough to satisfy new distributers. If you join a network marketing company, purchase product, see that your upline paid on your purchase, but you still haven't received your product, you may quit, and ask for a refund. New companies have a hard time keep up.

According to Robert Kiyosaki, it is not necessarily true that it takes money to make money but in this case, it is.

"How will I know about a company before anybody else" you ask? How can I get connected into the pipeline and filter out the rubbish when everybody says that their company is the best?

Well, that is a tough one because you must conduct your own research and you must find sources from different places. Honestly its damn near impossible in this day and age to be in the right place at the right time, however a small percentage of you will be in the right place at the right time right now! So, you need to ensure the MLM Company you associate with meets your requirements if you are to build that lifelong income.

Keep in mind, to be successful in the long run, you must be satisfied a company will meet all of these requirements not just some of them. Each and every one of them! How many companies truly do fit all of these requirements? Before we talk about the right company, let us discover the most booming, growing, and profitable industry, which is almost recession proof. That's right – Wellness – the industry that can be an unstoppable cash flow for you.

I was diagnosed 5 1/2 yrs. ago with rheumatoid arthritis and it hit me like a big concrete block. I was only 47....Over the next 5 yrs. I have had horrible pain, swelling, and been on all kinds of meds. The swelling was horrible. Now, I have not taken a single arthritic medicine or injection since I started Zija. I have no swelling, no pain. Not only that...and without trying at all, I have lost 17 pounds! Vicki C., Lexington, KY

A closer look at Moringa and Zija

Now that we have covered network marketing and what Wellness industry brings to the table, let us take a few minutes to go back to Moringa. The cultivation of Moringa is booming in Nigeria. However, the demand for it is still not met. Moringa is a high demand low volume product now, which costs more than a barrel of crude oil.

Can you make money from Moringa? Absolutely YES! The market is evergreen and you can make good money from the sale of Moringa products such as seeds, oil, tea, capsules, powder, etc.

However, what is a good way to get the best out of Moringa and make money? Should you cultivate your own Moringa trees? That depends on the time, money, and efforts you can spend. Moreover, there are some uncontrollable factors such as climate, environment, and soil which determine whether you can cultivate it or not.

I started taking Zija in March of 2009. The first thing I noticed was the absence of joint pain. Next, I noticed that I was sleeping better at night and that my restless leg problems stopped. I have also noticed an improvement in my eye sight. Last but not least my energy level and a sense of wellness have improved. Zija works! Glen R. – Buffalo, KY

Luckily, there are supplements available in the market, which are still niche and sparsely available. Yet you can sell it to make money.

Zija is the most prominent player in the market when it comes to offering Moringa supplements. Zija offers delicious, all-natural beverage made from Moringa, which offers same nutrients and benefits as received by consuming the plant raw. Effectively, Zija offers cell-ready nutrients, antioxidants, minerals, omega oils and vital proteins. Moreover, Zija is the first company to commercialize and bring into light Moringa's nutritional properties. Consuming Moringa raw may not appeal to many taste buds; however, Zija is refreshing, tasty yet helps in maintaining a healthy, active, and nourishing lifestyle. It brings a blend of nature and balance.

This drink is 100% natural, Halal, and Kosher certified, which contains 90 verifiable nutrients in each of its servings. Each of the servings consists of the proprietary blend of organically grown Moringa tree, fruit, and seed.

Zija works on a direct distribution model, popularly known as network marketing. This business model helps people to run independent business with fewer overhead costs, which helps in passing the savings to you, the independent agent or distributer.

Zija is perfect for making money for:

1. Health conscious people who wish to get Moringa products for free
2. People interested in creating a stream of money
3. Serious entrepreneurs who wish to make some serious money and gain their financial freedom

As a Zija distributer or business owner, people have successfully learned to earn 6-figure incomes – people from background such as home moms, business owners, students, teachers, etc.

If someone is looking for a weight management program or simply a nutritional supplement, you will be happy to learn that Zija's Moringa products will really help. Business owners and distributers have full freedom to sell the products the way they like. They can even use Zija's name.

Moreover, each sale is followed by a commission paid for the cost of one month supply and a includes a money back guarantee for the purchaser, which is not very common for any business model or product whatsoever.

Zija's products speak for themselves. They are not like other medications that may have side effects or are more of a bluff or rely on the placebo effect, these are real, peer tested products. The biggest success factor with Zija's model is that it shares its profits with its distributers along with the regular commissions. Perhaps this is the biggest testament to its large network of distributers since no other network marketing company offers this in the same way.

Zija's training workshops have some of the top trainers from the network marketing industry. Moreover, they have a simple duplicable system, which can be replicated irrespective of someone's qualification or experience.

There are hundreds of ways to generate leads while working as an entrepreneur with Zija. Simply put, if you love socializing, this will reap benefits. If you are on Facebook, Twitter, YouTube, or LinkedIn; or if you like networking, advertising, partnering with people; or if you like team work, nothing can stop you from your financial freedom. It is raining leads and if you do not get one, you are not looking.

What's next? It is important to understand why you should get involved in leveraging the network marketing model in the first place. It is important to note here that people love social recommendations. We all socialize whether it is face to face, at office, in our neighborhood, or online. If this looks familiar, let us come to the next chapter.

I began taking the Zija products in November of 2009 due to having had three operations on my ankles as the result of accidents; and by having a spinal fusion I developed severe arthritis and back pain. I have been drinking Zija smart mix and taking the XM3 caps each day. The results have been a loss of 14 lbs. without any type of exercise and I have gained lots of energy from the drink. Donnie B., – Hodgenville, KY

Top Earner in Zija and his story:

David Moses – Zija International Top Earner

David Moses is the first Zija Crown Diamond Elite, and their top income earner. He was on stage recently receiving a $3,000,000 check. But don't let the money fool you, he's a very humble man.

Married, with 2 children, David lives in Toronto, Canada. He found networking through an ad in a free newspaper, that was sitting in a government unemployment office. Starting with a referral from his Mom, he made his way to becoming the networking success that become today.

That was a long time ago, and one of the lessons he learned was to NOT get involved in 'new' or 'unfunded' companies. They don't last. That's why he was so happy to find Zija. He says (of Zija management 'I wanted to be associated with that kind of track record, because I had never failed to build an organization, companies had always failed me.'

Zija at this moment in time is ready for growth, feels David 'obviously if we are in a company that is growing then we too can grow with that company. If we are in a company that is shrinking then it is difficult to grow when the walls are coming down. ZIJA has gone from less than 500k per month in sales in Sept 2009 to more than $11.5 million per month as of November 2012.'

For those looking for a serious place to create their life time residual income, Zija is ready for that kind of growth and can take a hard worker with it. David says Zija will double pervious sales in 2013 that 'will make us the fastest growing company relative to our size in 2013'.

What is the secret of this Zija multimillion dollar earner? '…never stopped building, I am always in prospecting and relationship building mode and always looking to help another person reach the next level. If we are constantly building others, empowering, inspiring, and advancing their success.......'.

If you follow that same success formula, of never stop building, you can find yourself following, or even surpassing David's incredible income story.

Zija – Filling the Gap between Wellness and Making Money

When a supplement pops out of nowhere and is featured in the media, as on the Dr. Oz Show, it is bound to attract some burning question like is it really worth the hype or not? We have already discussed about the power of Moringa Oleifera and how it is amazing as a superfood. Moreover, companies have solidly claimed that it is all set to explode its demand in the wellness industry.

Superfoods are big business

The term 'superfoods' is often used for blueberries, acai berries, goji berries, green tea, etc depending on who is claiming what. However, there are some critical factors consumers consider before they even buy anything labeled as 'superfood'.

One is relevant scientific proof to back up the claims. For instance, if Food X mitigates diabetes and Y reduces cancerous cells yet there is no scientific proof to back it up, consumers will think twice before consuming it.

Second, the availability of 'superfood' is also a critical factor driving its demand. Foods such as blueberries are easily available in the market. Yet, there are other superfoods, which are specialty items and are only available through a few supplement makers.

Since drinking Zija I have noticed an incredible reduction in allergy and sinus problems. It is something I have battled for years and treated with shots, medicine, and herbal remedies. None of those have been near as effective as Zija to take care of my symptoms.

My 9 year old son is seeing benefits with his allergies from drinking the product as well. The natural energy is amazing! It lasts all day. Jonathan M. - Bowling Green, KY

Moringa oleifera

We have already discussed how Moringa Oleifera is touching the lives of millions and how all of its claims are scientifically proven. Moreover, it is perhaps one of those supplements, which has literally no side effects.

Moreover, Moringa Oleifera has a sky rocketing demand since it is not easily available anywhere. Today, the world faces one of the biggest challenges that adversely affect our health and well-being. While we have abundant food and dieticians around us, we are not getting proper nutrition to supplement our body. Obesity has infested the world and millions of people globally are desperate to shed some pounds. It is time for a change and Moringa is the change.

In the light of the increasing demand and the benefits Moringa brings to the table, Zija International is making a change in the market.

I had severe pain in both knees. I had allergies, and asthma. Not only have I lost 37 lbs., but I have no knee pain, no allergies and no asthma. I also had a hyper-active 12 year old son who's very smart but was not living up to his potential. Now he is leveled out and an A student. Jennifer L., Munfordville, KY

The Zija Story

Zija International is a multi-million dollar network marketing company that houses tens of thousands of independent distributers and consumers worldwide. Zija is an official distributer of Moringa based products in the market and is bridging the demand-supply gap for Moringa.

The company has quickly become an industry leader experiencing remarkable growth, doubling every year. Its success story begins with one man discovering a tree grown in faraway lands, that man was Ken Brailsford. A pioneer in the nutritional supplement industry, he's known as the father of herbal incapsulation and now founder of Zija International.

Ken was happily retired until a friend called him up and wanted to show him a video that he had recorded off of the Discovery Channel he wanted him to get into business. Initially Ken declined. However, when he watched the video on Moringa oleifera he knew by the time it was finished he had to be involved with it. It was something that was great and the world needed, and he felt impressed and spiritually prompted that this is something he had to do. And so he became involved with his friend in a business venture that would change the lives of countless people throughout the world.

Ken approached biochemists, scientists, and pharmacologists around the world to learn as much as he could from them. He even worked closely with Dr. Monica Marcu, a veteran botanical researcher and clinical pharmacologist and other visionaries to develop ways to boost Moringa's amazing benefits. Thus began the drive to create Moringa-based products including energy drinks, nutritionals, weight management system, and a line of skin care products.

As you have read throughout this book, Zija and Moringa are changing the lives of millions with positive individual experiences.

Tina is 73 year old, has diabetes, and has a cholesterol level of 197. Tina tried a lot of supplements and medications for a healthy life but most of her efforts did not yield the desired results. Tina then tried Zija's Moringa supplement. In a few months, her cholesterol level went down to 160. She lost significant weight and has good health by choice.

These are few people who have benefitted from Zija's Moringa. The list of people making money through Zija is also equally exhaustive. No matter what level of experience you have, Zija provides an outstanding opportunity to build your own highly profitable business. The combination of the right product, the right timing and the right pay plan make Zija truly special.

How Ken Brailsford and Zija got started

Really important to Ken, is the fact that Moringa is a nourisher, a healer, a beautician, a dietician, and a humanitarian. The health benefits of Moringa are truly amazing. But perhaps the most amazing thing about Moringa is the hundreds of research articles that have been published in just the last few years. Ken enlisted the help of Russ Bianchi world renowned scientist, food formulator and President of Adept Solutions a leading global product development and formulation firm.

Russ began creating new ways to maximize Moringa's health benefits. The result is Zija's extensive line of products including nutritional drink mixes nutritional energy drinks a complete weight loss and management system and an innovative skin care line. Each one of these products provide all of Moringa's over 90 verifiable benefits including cell ready vitamins, minerals, vital proteins antioxidants, and omega oils.

Zija's Moringa trees are grown on proprietary farms in dry hot climates where they thrive. The trees, organically raised without chemicals, are harvested carefully by hand then shade dried, insuring that essential nutrients remain intact. Unlike other Moringa products on the market Zija uses all of the most nutrient, rich parts of the tree the leaves, the seeds, and the fruit.

I have been drinking Zija Smart Mix for going on 4 months now and went to the eye doctor yesterday and my eyesight has improved. My prior prescription was - 1.50 in both eyes and now it is -.75 in one eye and - 1.00 in the other! I also suffer from severe allergies and since drinking Zija I haven't had a problem at all with my allergies. This is the first Spring in years that I haven't had to take any allergy medication! Peggy H., - Somerset, KY

Rod Larsen - President and CEO of Zija International

Rod Larsen understands the essence of building a long term lasting bond not only with his family but also passing this to the masses. He is helping people achieve and succeed in what he sees are the four pillars of a successful life, that he called 'Life Unlimited': Nutrition, having Financial Freedom, an Active Lifestyle and also Personal Development. Rod, through Zija, provides people with tools and framework they need to succeed. Unlike other products that require heavy marketing, promotion, shipping, etc. Zija is different. It is in its own league.

Merely plugging the system that exists with individual contribution can help anyone achieve high level of success and influence and enjoyment with Zija.

Considering the booming wellness industry, the benefits of Moringa, and Zija one could not be surprised to hear Zija' Moringa product is the ultimate answer to bring this nutritional superfood to the consumers. At the same it, the men and woman helping to make this happen are achieving their financial dreams. Their long term success is no longer a distant reality.

Pam S., featured in NBC's Biggest Losers has been a big fan of Zija. She has struggled to lose weight and as she said it is really hard to say "no to food." After her frustration for years, she decided to try Zija's XM4 capsules. She was doing the same thing before and after one month, she lost 10 lbs and 4 ½ inches off her waist. The capsules made her not want food, she doesn't think about it, doesn't crave it, yet it gives her miraculous energy to stay fit.

If you would like to own your business, spend more time with friends and family, stay healthy and active, travel the world, lose weight, yet create huge profits, Zija is the right answer.

By associating with Zija, you will be a part of a turnkey business model. Moreover, you will get access to easy-to-use tools, support, and one of the most attractive compensations in the market. Associating with health and wellness industry gives you a potential of tapping the next trillion-dollar economic sector, which will create more millionaires than ever before.

In mid-January 2009 I was hospitalized with chest pains, I am a diabetic and my elevated glucose levels were out of control, it took them 4 days and numerous tests and insulin injections to get it regulated and somewhat normal. I was sent home with a hand full of prescriptions, three diabetic medications, including insulin I had to inject daily, blood pressure meds, and cholesterol meds. Mid-August I started consuming Zija, and mid-September I began the weight management system. I've lost nearly 40 pounds, tossed all but 2 of my medications haven't had an insulin shot in months, and have more energy than I've had in years." Neil N., - Hardyville, KY

How Zija's is Helping People Achieve Their Financial Dreams

Zija manufactures products from its Utah facility. They use cutting edge technology, which results in product of the highest quality. Not only does it provide an amazing business opportunity for anyone looking for financial independence but also nutrient rich product. Moreover, the company provides amazing tools and benefits to help its distributers succeed. Many of Zija independent distributers are already millionaires. It is truly Life Unlimited and profit for each of the distributers who are making it happen.

Zija's nutritional line offers two prime products – SmartDrink and SmartMix. SmartMix is an open packet to which water can added to provide an easy dose of Moringa nutrition. Zija is the only company to offer the nutritional value of Moringa in a nourishing and tasty form. Their weight management system utilizes the benefits of Moringa to help in weight loss. The weight management system includes XMam, XMpm, XM+, SmartMix, and Premium Tea.

Zija also offers a power packed energy dream called XM3 Drink, which consists of all natural ingredients including caffeine, desert tea, green tea, fruit pectin, TMG organic, Ginseng, and Allium sativum.

The company also offers anti-aging natural skin treatment system through its anti-aging night repair, a daily moisturizer, a spa masque, a rehydrating mist, eye serum, Zija oil, and a daily cleanser. Each of the products has been formulated by Zija's team of experts.

After drinking Zija for one month, the pain in my hands, back and legs disappeared. Six weeks later, I noticed my blood sugar had dropped and was staying between 95-120. Before I began drinking Zija it tested anywhere from 180-190. The only thing that had changed in my diet was the Zija. I decided to do my own experi-

ment. I thought maybe I just wanted it to work well for me, so, I went off of Zija for one month. The pain in my hands, back and legs came back. Not only my pain returned, but my blood sugar spike 40 points and almost returned to the high level it was before I began to drink Zija. I began drinking Zija again and taking the XM3 capsules. I now have more energy than I have ever had before. I am on Zija for life!! Carol C., — Sebree, KY

The Zija Moringa Business Model

Zija offers several ways to make money. To get started as a distributer, you'd need to start with a distributer kit and the initial product. After that, you will need to maintain a monthly auto-ship of Zija's products. You can sell the products and/or sponsor people who purchase or sell products to earn income. Further, you can get added bonuses to that for your sales and productivity.

Leveraging a combined experience of 50 years, the Zija's thought leadership brings a proven brand and success to its distributers. When you join Zija, you join as a distributer under a mentor. Your mentor can help you to get started with business and help generate leads and prospects.

Let's look at Zija's business model:

Ways To Earn Income With Zija

DIRECT SALES

Earn income by purchasing product at wholesale price and selling it at retail price. You keep the profit.

FIRST ORDER BONUS (FOB)

Receive a 10-20% Bonus (up to $100) when your personally sponsored Distributers place a first-time order.

BUILDER BONUS

As a Qualified Active 150 Distributer, you earn a $30 Builder Bonus each time a personally sponsored Distributer reaches the rank of Builder.

VOLUME ORDER REBATE (VOR)

When your PV exceeds 250 in any one period, you will receive up to a 10% personal rebate on your PV greater than 250. And when one of your personally sponsored Distributers does the same, you'll receive up to 10% rebate on their PV greater than 250!

TEAM COMMISSIONS

The team commission gives you the benefit of being placed in one of two legs in your sponsor's group. You are compensated based on being qualified with at least one personally sponsored Active Distributers on your left and right leg. And, if you and two personally sponsored Distributers are Active 75 status, you will earn the rank of Builder and qualify for up to 15% in Team Commissions.

LEADERSHIP CHECK MATCH (LCM)

82 Max Hailey

At the Senior leadership level, you can earn a check match bonus based on a percentage of Team Commissions of the people you personally enroll, the people they enroll, and so on. You can earn LCM on up to 8 generations.

DIAMOND POOL

We have reserved up to 4% of the company's total commissionable Group Volume for qualified Diamond Executives.

MULTIPLE BUSINESS CENTERS

As your organization expands, you can essentially sponsor yourself by adding additional Business Centers. You may insert your new centers anywhere in your organization.

Tools and Perks

TEAM BENZ: Zija's luxury car program puts you behind the wheel like never before. If you "Qualify for the Ride", you'll get a cash bonus to put toward buying or leasing your own Mercedes Benz. You can earn from $400 - $1,000 per Period, based on Pay Rank.

ZIJA UNIVERSITY: Zija University is an incredible resource for those interested in learning how to start and run their own profitable business. We have organized video tutorials, training documents, and marketing materials into four easy courses: Orientation, Communications, Marketing 101, and Business Building. Class is now in session!

TEAM 250: TEAM 250 was established to help you grow your Zija business using a unique, zero-overhead, easily duplicable scenario. TEAM stands for Train, Enroll, remain Active and Qualified, and continually Motivate. Each time you qualify for TEAM 250, Zija will pay for your AutoShip, meaning you'll get free products just for building your business! You'll also get other privileges, including the opportunity to earn more money and TEAM 250 VIP access at Zija Corporate events.

ZIJA INCENTIVE PROGRAM (ZIP): The Zija Incentive Program (ZIP) was created to reward you for your hard work. You'll earn Incentive Points for specific tasks, and then you get to decide how to spend them! Do you want to see the world aboard a Zija Cruise? Attend International Convention or one of their Regional conferences.

Does anyone know what it is like to walk again? No pain! No pain at all! So, now I can walk. It is so wonderful. Does anyone know how long I have tried to lose weight? 40 years, 3 in wheelchair, so I gained more weight. Do you know, no one has asked me in 9 months, "are you diabetic?" The swelling is gone, the puffy face is thinner and my dimples are back! WOW! I love my Zija! Nancy de M.

Earning Wealth with Zija using the right Network Marketing strategies

Joining the wellness industry with Zija will be among the best decisions you will ever take. To top this decision with profits, here are the top steps from Zija's top marketing leaders in the industry, which will help you to steadfast with your business to earn profits!

Step 1-Work on Yourself

You are not successful if you have a great upline, you are successful if you ARE a great upline!

There is no question that the place to start with any successful network marketing recruiting program is with you. You are the foundation of your network marketing business. If you've been moderately successful in your network marketing recruiting efforts to date, but want to go much further in your team building, you already know how important it is to do a self-check on your beliefs, thoughts, emotions, language, energy vibration, and intentions before you interact with anyone. After all, everyone you talk with is a prospect for your business and/or knows someone who might be interested in your venture. Keep your personality free of 'weeds', such as allowing fear that you won't succeed in your network marketing business to degrade your confidence. If you do experience fear, admit to it, immediately pinpoint its source and identify the appropriate action remedy to conquer it.

For example, if you're afraid your up-and coming leaders aren't sufficiently committed to building their teams, redouble your commitment to them and communication with them to solidify your business-building partnership, but keep recruiting. Let them see you are leading by example.

Be honest about your reality. If your financial abundance is going in the wrong direction, assess your short-term and long-term risk and get help from a business coach or mentor who understands your business to help you make rapid course corrections with a realistic plan to turn around your network marketing business. Don't give yourself an 'out' by associating with friends or relatives or other network marketing entrepreneurs who use excuses, such as, "The economy is hitting everyone hard", or "network marketing" is in a state of decline in all of North America." Successful people rise above that type of limited thinking. Don't be lured into the state of mediocrity that keeps the masses stuck in place.

Allot at least 15 minutes per day for your ongoing personal development. Your personal growth is never done if you're committed to lifelong success.

I have been doing the XM3 drink and the smart mix since last October. I have lost 17 lbs. My husband is a diabetic; his blood sugar has dropped 150 points. He was taking ibuprofen due to arthritis in his back and he no longer takes that and no longer has back pain. Margaret B., – Albany, KY

Step 2—Work with Your Upline

The multilevel marketing business model is based on people helping people achieve their goals. Therefore building relationships up and down your organization is the second most important skill you need to hone, right alongside recruiting and launching new distributers. If you already have a strong relationship with your upline sponsor, then let them know on a regular basis, both privately and publicly, how much you appreciate their bringing you into their business. Don't take it for granted that your sponsor will automatically feel recognized and appreciated by you. Express your appreciation on a regular basis – they can be a big help to you!

If you don't currently have a strong relationship with your upline sponsor, look at why this is the case. Something about them attracted you in the first place to join them in their business.

What is Zija? What is in Zija? What is Moringa?   87

Sometimes a sponsor quits, moves away and loses touch or becomes inactive. If this is the case for you, then go up another level and contact your sponsor's sponsor in order to develop a strong working relationship with them. You might have to go up several levels until you make a good connection. Never blame lack of sponsor support for your lack of success. It's your responsibility to establish the best connection possible with an active distributer who is above you in rank. With your upline connection locked down, share your goals in writing with your sponsor on a quarterly basis and request regular telephone coaching from them to support you in achieving those goals. This is not a sign of weakness; rather it's a sign of strength. Your sponsor would wish that all of their team was like you!

Your sponsor can't grow their business without knowledge of what their team members are doing to grow their respective legs of the business. You and your sponsor are modeling the nature of symbiotic relationships that must be built in order for network marketing professionals to succeed. The nature of an network marketing business model is that you and those above and below you in your lineage are dependent on each other for your aggregate success. You can't expect your downline distributers to regularly communicate and work with you unless you demonstrate the importance of the distributer-to-sponsor connection. Lead by example.

BE the upline you wish you had!

Your distributers will do what you do in all facets of your network marketing business.

Step 3-Work with Your Downline

Eventually you can have thousands of distributers creating your income, and you'll need to engage with your team members in various ways. You've probably heard the expression, "Work with the willing", during the course of your network marketing leadership training. We suggest that being 'willing' isn't a strong enough requirement to earn your personal coaching time. Instead, work with those 'in action.'

If you haven't learned by now, you will learn soon enough that you can't motivate anyone to get into action with their network marketing business. As much as you love or like someone and see all kinds of potential in them, your time should be spent with those on the move, i.e. distributers who are consistently meeting new people, sharing third-party tools, presenting the business, and attending events.

You have much better odds of duplicating yourself as a leader with someone who is already showing initiative. Wouldn't you rather coach a player on the field as opposed to a fan sitting in the bleachers?

Hint: look for distributers who refer to their recruits as "my team" as a sign that they see themselves as business builders.

Each month, pick three up-and-coming leaders 'in action' and offer to personally coach them to their next rank advancement, and require them to do the same with their key people. This is a win/win/win scenario because you're helping them advance, you're helping them develop their leadership and duplication skills with their downline, and you're building your organization through duplication.

Many leaders have experimented with both weekly 30-minute team coaching calls and 5- minute daily individual coaching calls for distributers in our downline who are ready to advance. Without question, the daily calls are best to keep your finger on the pulse with each of your three builders for the 30-day coaching period. The 30 days pass quickly and there's no time for procrastination or excuses with daily contact.

You can find free conference calling services if you search Google or your favorite search engine.

What is Zija? What is in Zija? What is Moringa?   89

Leaders also don't recommend you provide 'carry over' coaching to the following month if a builder does not make their advancement goal. This policy creates a sense of urgency to get the job done in the 30-day period, operating with the joint belief that anything is possible! This type of monthly rank advancement coaching program raises your awareness of how and who you're investing your time with in your downline in order to recruit through duplication. It also highlights the value of your time to your entire downline, so any would-be builders understand they must earn your one-on-one time by first getting into action on their own.

The product has done some amazing things for me. I have been consuming the smart drink for 14 months, I have been off my diabetes meds for 8 months, my blood pressure meds for a year, and my joint pain in my shoulder has been virtually eliminated. David E., – Munfordville, KY

Step 4–Make a New General Prospect List

Entrepreneurs like a challenge, so here it is! It's time to step up your personal recruiting with a new list of 100 fresh Prospects. Take out your blank prospect forms and imagine it's day one of your network marketing business. Start writing names of people you've never contacted about your business.

The advantage of starting with a blank slate after you've been prospecting for a while is you can approach your business in a new light as an experienced recruiter. You might learn that you don't have 100 new names to put on your prospect forms, so it's time to get out and meet some new people! Try some new experiences to rapidly expand your network.

Give yourself one month to create your brand new 100-name prospect list and work it like you just started your networking business as a new distributer. Let your team know about your recruiting project and have fun with the process. It is recommend that you do this every six months to keep your network growing, your recruiting skills sharp, and your business fun factor high.

90   Max Hailey

I have been consuming Zija and XM3 for 6 weeks. I am a Diabetic and have high blood pressure. Both are maintaining a normal state. I have not taken my medication in two weeks, my feet no longer hurt, have energy, clearer mind, and no pain in wrist and back. I have lost 21.5 pounds. Love it!"   Kerry I.,- Fort Meyers, FL

Step 5–Create a List of 10 Influencers

Influencers are natural team builders because they're charismatic types who naturally attract others with their energy, love of life, wit, and action-oriented personality. It's a smart recruiting tactic for your networking business to create a list of 10 Influencers (separate from your list of new 100 Prospects) to expose to your business. Even one Influencer on your team can supercharge your growth.

Here is a super-secret tip that is perfect for Zija recruiters.

There are many doctors in big cities that are not practicing, or, due to immigration waits, are not allowed to practice. Some are just not interested in a regular practice. Some are hard at work on their practice but not doing well. You job is to just recruit one, and to work with them until they are highly successful on their own. Then you recruit another one for your other leg.

How is that news? Well, here is the secret strategy: You create mini events, seminars, on various topics. Could be weight loss, could be lower blood pressure, or even nutrition and fatigue. Get a small location that is not expensive, a local school at night, etc., and put out flyers for 3 weeks all over the local areas. Hit the gyms, medical centers, parking lots of the gyms and medical centers, blanked the area.

On the evening of the meeting, you do the introductions. Your doctor does a seminar on the topic, with about 30% about presentation being about how Zija is perfect to solve this concern. You get up after, and explain that Zija is not available at local health food stores but only thought a network of Zija distributers. Sadly, you say, there are not enough, and you are looking for more. It's very lucrative you say, and it helps people, people just like you!

And this is the clincher: Each will be in the downline of the doctor, who will act as their local product celebrity.

Explain it's getting late, and you are taking a 5 minute break, for those would just want to buy some Zija products, (back of the room), and for those who would like to stay and see a short presentation on how to make money offering Zija, stick around, as you, (or your sponsor) is going to explain, and guess what, each of you will be sponsored in Dr. X's team, 'wont that be great, having a Dr. as your sponsor?'

Let us take another example of a 'High I' or Influencer called Bruce, who is not a doctor, he can be from any vocational background. He wakes up with a big smile on his face and doesn't put it away until he falls asleep at night. Bruce is highly valued by his upline sponsor because he personally sponsored dozens of distributers during his first year in his MLM business and continues to do so as a team leader. He is also highly valued by his downline distributers because they feed off his energy and optimism to move them into accelerated action.

Influencers can come from any profession, although you're more apt to find them in sales, coaching, and teaching fields where they enjoy creating excitement and promotions related to their field. They thrive on continuously meeting new people and positively affecting others' lives. Their energy also makes them excellent candidates to start a part-time networking business alongside their full-time job until they make the transition to being a full-time networking professional. Once an Influencer gets a taste of the freedom, fun, adventure, and unlimited growth potential of an networking business, and they're with the right company with products that align with their passions and interests, they'll feel motivated to be a change agent and dynamic leader in their company.

As Bruce says, "I was born to be a network marketer!" His prior careers as a teacher, counselor, and real estate broker (to name a few) were fun and satisfying for a time, but his networking business promises to keep him challenged indefinitely.

Sponsoring an Influencer is like buying a thoroughbred race horse. You need to give them a lot of freedom to learn on their own and enjoy the adventurous aspects of an network marketing business. They aren't afraid of making mistakes, and they thrive on competition. Once you get two Influencers in a team building mode in your downline, consider having them compete against each other to create even more growth and excitement for them and your team!

My mom has lost 24 pounds, she is off of 2 out of 3 diabetes medications, and her thyroid, which was growing A type Cells are no longer there! My dad has lost 16 pounds and has lowered his blood pressure. My husband who has lost a pant size. And for me, I've dropped a pant size as well, cut back my blood pressure medication and off my prevacid (Acid Reflux Med)! Debbie M.

Step 6–Create a List of 10 Prospects Above You on the Socioeconomic Scale

If you're like most networking recruiters, you're a lot more comfortable contacting people who you consider to be equal to or beneath your socioeconomic status. We're going to challenge you to prospect 'up' the socioeconomic chain by making a list of 10 Successful Entrepreneurs (separate from your new list of 100 new Prospects and 10 Influencers), who you might previously have prejudged as unfit prospects for your MLM business. You may have told yourself these Successful Entrepreneurs were too busy, too successful, too imbedded in their current business, or too wealthy to meet with you. Those are the exact names you need to put on your list of 10 Successful Entrepreneurs.

These Successful Entrepreneurs can be among your strongest prospects because:

* Successful people are usually open to learning about new opportunities;

* You don't know the truth of their socioeconomic status from external trappings;

* You're going to be moving up on the socioeconomic chain as your MLM business grows, so it would behoove you to practice interacting with people in that sphere;

* Your competitors have probably already introduced them to other MLM companies and they could be on the verge of joining another MLM company; you'll want to educate them on what's unique about your business;

* They know other Successful Entrepreneurs to whom they can introduce you, which can help you whether or not they decide to partner with you in your business;

* Successful Entrepreneurs are networking masters and have large, established networks, which enable them to build a team with a lot more ease than most others launching an networking business;

* They can teach you and your team skills that will help everyone grow bigger and faster;

* They would be interested in what business gurus, including Donald Trump, Robert Kiyosaki, and Paul Zane Pilzer, teach about the benefits for anyone to grow an networking income stream.

Life truly does begin when you leave your comfort zone. Put no limits on yourself in terms of who you'll invite to join you in your business. Proceed with professional dignity and share what could be the most exciting entrepreneurial venture to date for your Successful Entrepreneur prospects!

Let me start by saying as a former athlete and catcher for 15 plus years I have suffered knee and back pain for quite some time. Even to the point of taking 8-10 ibuprofen a day and still not getting much relief. Last year I started on blood pressure meds due to slightly elevated blood pressure from many of the stresses of everyday life. I am most excited to share that I recently had a complete blood work done and was able to compare it to one from exactly a year ago. I am excited to see in black and white some of the positive results from consuming Zija since Oct. My total choles-terol went from 181 to 154, triglycerides 128 to 73, LDL/HDL ratio went from 2.6 to 2.2 and I am also no longer on blood pressure meds and nothing for joint or back pain. I am so thankful for the friend and now my business partner that introduced me to Zija."
Chris R., - Hodgenville, KY

Step 7–Create a Foolproof Recruiting System

Hopefully your new prospecting lists are created or well underway and your excitement is building for this next recruiting phase to grow your networking business. Unless your mind works like a file cabinet, you'll need a foolproof system to help you manage your recruiting process.

Chances are, like many, you've tried various follow-up systems with mixed results. Successful leaders have started with paper lists, index cards, spreadsheets, databases, and various other methods to capture new contact information and track our recruit-ing activity with each prospect. Typically, after about one month or less, each system collapsed, primarily because the daily details of contacting 12 to 20 people by phone, social media, email, or in person fell through the cracks.

What is Zija? What is in Zija? What is Moringa?   95

One foolproof system works like this. Each person on your prospecting list has a separate sheet of copy paper filed alphabetically in a three-ring binder. If you have their business card, then scan the card and that is printed at the top of the page. If you don't have their business card, handwrite their name and any pertinent contact information at the top of the page. In this day of Facebook messaging, you can reach a lot of people by just having their Facebook url.

Review your recruiting activities at the end of each work day to gauge the activities for the day and the next day. Note each and every prospect on their individual page. Do not close your discussion on any prospect unless you decide and note your next step in recruiting process with them. On the outside of the notebook, maintain a running list of specific names, dates, and activities on the schedule and lists of prospects who have been tagged with a general follow-up timeframe, such as 'next week' or 'early next month.'

From the running list, create a new task list for each workday based on the follow ups or new contacts planned for that day. With this system, if you don't meet at the end of the work day to review the events of the day and note future contact activities, you'll have to allow for additional time at the morning meeting on the following workday to complete both the daily review and the new day's plan.

For closure, it's best to have the prospecting meeting at the end of each work day before you call it a wrap. Of course, all of the contacts' information is stored electronically along with appointments. The external, manual system allows you to make lots of details on each contact and ensure you're clear on your next step. It's the very rare entrepreneur who can build a multi-million dollar a year business without help, so if you don't already have an assistant, when you can afford it, hire one to help you with this all-important team-building function. Once again, turn to a outsourcer in a country where $75 per week is a good wage.

My uncle in Indiana was diagnosed with diabetes a few months ago. Since he has been on Zija about 3 months, he has lost 20 lbs., went to the doctor the other day and he is off all his medications....blood pressure, cholesterol, and sugar pill...another great testimony but when it is your family it means that much more...let Zija change your family's life! Carley F.

Step 8-Present with Intention

No matter who you approach as a prospect for your MLM business, you'll want to set a strong intention to learn about their needs, convert them as a customer or distributer (ideally coach them to convert themselves), or at the very least, obtain qualified referrals from them. A qualified referral is one they're willing to introduce you to with a call or three party meeting.

Emphatic language and proven scripts can help you communicate your intention in a professional manner. Take advantage of all the training your company and sponsor provide in the area of prospecting scripts. Regarding scripts: Many people report that they got off to a fast start with their networking recruiting using the proven script provided by their sponsor. After a few months, they were so smart, they abandoned the script, and their conversions dropped.

Don't reinvent the wheel; use what works! Soon you'll master the art of conversing with your prospects by using all the key points and flow of your script while at the same time sounding natural and personable.

Always ask your different uplines for scripts. Become a script collector. You may find some that adapt better to your personality, or to a 'type' of prospect.

When you speak with any prospect ask a lot of questions and keep the spotlight on them and their needs. Find out what's missing in their life (e.g., extra time, money, social life, autonomy) and steer your presentation to help them feel the difference between their

What is Zija? What is in Zija? What is Moringa? 97

current life and what's possible for them and how it would make them feel to achieve their dreams if they were successful in an networking business of their own.

I began taking the Weight Management System and in a little over 6 months I'm taking none of my Metformin (2000mg a day)! I no longer have to take my BP medicine and I've lost 46 lbs! We now give Zija to all three of our kids and my daughter drinks the XM3 drink before basketball games. My youngest son's pediatrician literally pulled my wife aside and asked her if we had changed doctors because my son (who used to frequent their office) hadn't been there in such a long time! We are literally Zija users "For Life"! C. B., Tennessee

There is a way to make use of what you learned from your prospect:

"Tom, remember when you told me you wanted to earn enough money to buy a boat? Were you serious, or just kidding around?"

Practice strong language that helps guide your prospect to a decision without a lot of confusion. For example, instead of describing the four different flavors of your health shake, say, "I recommend the chocolate flavor because it's the most popular and if you don't like it I will help you change it on your subsequent order." Remember, the confused mind says, "No", so offer few and simple choices in order to move your prospect to action.

When you receive objections, such as, "I have no time" or "I have no money", they are clues that you haven't connected with your prospect emotionally and allowed them to naturally reach their own conclusions about how your MLM business could help them. Why? Because those are the two chief reasons why someone would begin a networking business with you.

Use objections as prompts to tell a heartfelt story and then ask a question. For example, when a prospect says they "have no time", simple say, "I thought I wouldn't have time either when I first heard about Zija, but, you know, I found that it doesn't require more than a few hours a week for me to create a better life for my family and I. I realized that if I didn't change, nothing would change for us. Would improving your life be worth a few extra hours a week to you? How would you feel if you were able to have more time to spend with your growing family?"

Keep control of your presentations with a strong intention of helping your prospects easily connect to the solutions you have to offer without rushing them or pressuring them in any way. The more they feel their decision was their idea, the more satisfied they will be with you as their 'decision coach' and with their experience with your products and/or business opportunity.

If you are 'pushy' they will be thinking, 'I can't let my warm market near this guy'.

Chasity S. was diagnosed with stage four cancer in November of 2009. I gave Chasity exactly 2 boxes of Zija plus 3 individual packs. Chasity took a half a pack of the Zija Smart mix and her father and brother drank the balance of what she had left over. Chasity underwent chemo therapy and had surgery that was to last four hours, the surgeon was going to remove as much of the softball sized tumor as he could, which had attached itself to the main artery of her heart, her liver, her kidney and her colon.

Step 9–Transform Recruiting from Work into Play

One of the easiest ways to sabotage yourself as an networking recruiter is to over think the process. If you catch yourself thinking more and doing less, it's time to inject more fun into your recruiting process! This often happens to those after a year. Keep to the basics!

Here are some suggestions for how to be a more playful recruiter:

What is Zija? What is in Zija? What is Moringa? 99

* Pick a different profession each month for your recruiting focus and enroll others on your team to do the same. For example, declare June 'Teachers Month' and talk to as many teachers as possible just as they're winding down their school year.

* Follow the commercial market and, for example, offer a product special for Cyber Monday after the Thanksgiving holiday. Contrary to what you might think, the holiday season is a wonderful time to continue your Zija recruiting because people are more open to everything during the holidays.

* Find the next community event that's soliciting vendors and set up a table for your business. Wear your company logo on your shirt, decorate your table with some colorful balloons and provide an enticing raffle item from your product line in order to collect contact information. Aim the prize to the prospects. For example, if you want to promote Zija's success at lowering blood pressure, offer a blood pressure monitor as a prize. You will get some serious names and phone numbers. It may cost you $60, but once you divide the cost per lead, you'll find it pretty inexpensive. Most importantly, smile at everyone you see. Take another distributer along for backup and camaraderie. Don't go with any expectation; just be open to who stops by your table and engage in light conversation. The more you make your business look like fun, the more people you'll attract to want to do what you do.

* If you have a dog, order a custom dog collar and leash with your company logo or product logo and take your dog to several dog parks in your area for some networking fun.

* Buy a present for yourself and give it to a loved one to hold for you along with the gift receipt. Set a recruiting goal for the week and if you make it, you get the gift; if you don't make your goal, your loved one returns the gift. Create a few more playful practices you can use in your Zija recruiting process to keep it fun!

Once the surgeon had opened her up he found the tumor was completely unattached from all her organs and was less than half the size of a golf ball. He was astounded! He completely searched the little girl's body for the tumor and to his great amazement it was gone! The side effects she was supposed to experience from the chemotherapy never happened! The surgeon said, "I have never seen a stage 4 tumor shrink like that!!" The Zija product is the best! I highly recommend it! Charles S.

Step 10 -Leverage Technology

Any smart Zija recruiter in today's world knows how to leverage technology for results. Unless you've been living under a rock for the past few years, you're probably active in some form of social media. The best advice we have for leveraging social media is to focus on Facebook. There are many fine Facebook consultants and training programs available. Remember, you're selling a freedom lifestyle with your Zija business along with your company's overall mission. Make sure your posts are in alignment with this important and powerful Zija marketing message.

We're able to leverage technology to grow our Zija business with a company provided mobile application to capture both product orders and new distributer applications when on-the-go. This one small, free application has proven its weight in gold for not leaving transactions to chance. Don't overlook technology tools such as these provided by your company.

Use in-person meetings, Skype, and Facetime for communicating with top producers in your downline and new promising prospects. E-newsletters, Webinars, events, and teleconference calls are best for large group communications with distributers and prospects. Your time is valuable; choose the technology that best fits your audience and your business goals.

I suggest you use an electronic spreadsheet to track all your recruiting activities, including calls, online messages, meetings, social media posts, product sample sharing, presentations, three-

What is Zija? What is in Zija? What is Moringa?   101

way calls, and even the 15 minutes per day you spend on your personal development. What you measure you can then manage and improve!

Make sure you continue to plan ahead for the right technology tools for your Zija business and include continuous technology upgrades in your annual budget.

Go back to the chapter on outsourcing and ask yourself how you can use the technology of the internet to outsource more tasks to people willing to take them on for you, so you can spend the saved time making more sales and building your team bigger.

My pastor's father has had 2 rounds with cancer. What we discovered through his experience was Zija helps the recovery time from chemo as well as enhances the effects of the drugs being used to attack the cancer. The tea is great, too, to help rid the body of the extra toxins. He has defeated cancer twice.   - Dick M., GA

Bottom Line on Zija Products:

One of the keys behind the success of Zija is the scientist and formulator of Zija's products, Russ Bianchi. A startling differences between Zija and other network marketing company's products is the fact that Zija took a much more 'holistic' approach to formulation. Typically a company looks for an 'active' or key ingredient in a fruit, vegetable, leaf or whatever. They analyze it and try and either extract it, or duplicate it in the laboratory.

This is not the case with Zija. 'Zija's beverage reflects exactly what is in the Moringa plant…it contains the entire Moringa plant including the leaf, seeds and fruit, and all of it organically grown and harvested' says formulator Bianchi. This 'holistic' approach means the 'whole' of the Moringa leaf is used, producing one of the most nutritionally dense and highest nutrient valued product of its nature. It is 'enzymatically alive and active', body recognizable, and 100% natural, adds Mr. Bianchi.

Ensuring that Zija has enough Moringa Leaf for its products would be a concern if not for the fact that Zija, actually manages its own organic Moringa farms. Owning and managing the raw material for a networking nutritional company is virtually unheard of. It allows them to product a 'premium-quality, pharmaceutical-grade nutritional beverage', boasts Bianchi. And so he should boast, pharmaceutical-grade products are extremely rare in the world of network marketing. Zija's products are literally the top of the line in quality and performance. Their commitment to quality is without par.

What benefits do you gain from Moringa and using Zija's products?

1) **Total Immune System Nourishment** – The body's vast immune system requires a continuous supply of building blocks from our daily food supply. If most of what we eat is junk or 'waste' – empty calories, our immune system is the first to feel it. Once that happens, we are open to opportunistic attack from all sources, from environmental to fungi, from viruses to inflammatory diseases like cancer, and many others. Zija's Moringa oleifera is one of the ultimate sources for all of the required building blocks of the immune system like vitamins, antioxidants, anti-inflammatories, minerals, and essential amino acids. Zija comes pre-loaded with all the required immunity boosters. This is why you read and hear about those with immune disease and cancers (inflammatory diseases) preach so much about Zija. It's not wishful thinking, its helping fight arthritis, MS, and much more.

2) **Cardiovascular Overhaul** – Significant peer reviewed research on Moringa oleifera and its effect on the circulatory, blood and cardiovascular systems is one of the reasons so many Zija users have reported stopping their blood pressure medications. Think of the potential of stopping cardiovascular diseases and deaths long before they were even a concern by regularly using Zija.

3) **Nutritional Delivery** – all of Zija's products are 100% bioavailable. Zija uses only all natural, organic raw materials to product the highest quality Moringa product you can purchase in so many countries. Unless you grew your own Moringa, in an organic setting, you pretty much don't have access to the quality Zija does.

4) **Moringa Battles Diabetes and Abnormal Blood Glucose Levels** - Sadly, the SAD diet, (Standard American Diet of refined flours, highly sugared or high fructose corn syrup sweetened and the microwaveable empty calorie sodium loaded manufactured food) is a dealing cause of diabetes, obesity, and abnormal blood glucose challenges. Moringa is full of a wide variety of nutrients that normalize blood sugar levels. This is one of the key reasons

you read of many diabetics eliminating their treatments after following a regular use of Zija.

5) A Nutritional Powerhouse delivery: Moringa used in Zija delivers: Vitamin A, (both Alpha and Beta-Carotene), B, B1, B2, B3, B6, B12, C, D, E, K, Folate or Folic Acid, Biotine, Minerals - Calcium, Chloride, Chromium, Copper, Fluorine, Iron, Manganese, Magnesium, Molybdenum, Phosphorus, Potassium, Sodium, Selenium, Sulfur, Zinc, as well as All 8 essential amino acids, Isoleucine, Leucine, Lysine, Methionine, Phenylalanine, Threonine, Tryptophan, and Valine. Additionally, you will find Zija's Moringa to have 10 other amino acids, Alanine, Arginine, Aspartic Acid, Cysteine, Glutamine, Glycine, Histidine, Proline, Serine, Tyrosine. Lastly, Zija has other beneficial nutrients, namely, Chlorophyll, Carotenoids, Cytokinins, Flavonoids, Omega 3, 6 And 9 Oils, Plant Sterols, Polyphenols, Lutein, Xanthins, and Rutlin to name only a few. Bottom line: Moringa oleifera is the most nutrient rich plant yet discovered.

6) Zija's Moringa offers both Anti-Aging and Anti-Inflammatory support and benefits. The powerful combination of the nutrients listed in point 5 help to protect the body's cells from some of the common conditions of again. Again, this is part of the general feedback of Wellness that users report once starting on Zija products. It's also the reason they stay on them. Some researches see cancer through the inflammatory lends. The jury is still out, but clearly, cancer suffers have reported some extraordinary remissions after using Zija products. There could be a multitude of cancers in many Zija users that never spread or are even noticed due to the regular consumption of Moringa.

7) Moringa delivers you a rich sources of 'living', bio-available enzymes. Lack of enzymes can appear as early as the mid-20's and is a leading cause of many disease. Zija's Moringa offers a rich array of unmodified enzymes with each sip. Books could be filled with the restorative power that enzymes bring. It's one of the major reasons that many Zija users report an overall 'general' feeling of rejuvenation.

8) **Z-Atin** – To quote Russ Bianchi: 'Z-ATIN includes A: Zeatin, a potent antioxidant, B: Quercitin, a flavonoid known for its ability to neutralize free radicals and relieve inflammation; C) Beta-Sitosterol, a nutrient superstar that blocks "Bad" (LDL) cholesterol formation for build-up and is an anti-inflammatory agent for the body; D) Caffeoylquinic Acid, another powerful anti-inflammatory compound for body benefit; and E) Kaempferol, a key nutrient that promotes healthy body cellular function.

Conclusion

Congratulations!

First off I'd like to thank you for reading this book and I hope that I have answered any questions you may have. If not please feel free to send me a personal email Max.Hailey@AllAmericanISP.com

I hope that you have read this book in the order I wrote it; but if you didn't, I encourage you to go back and do so.

There are many, many different companies out there, obviously some are huge and well known and some so new and tiny that even I haven't heard of them yet. Remember the earlier section on timing? Timing is HUGE! I can't stress that enough, so let me repeat that...timing is HUGE! I'm not going to pad this section repeating what I said earlier but just remember the importance of timing.

Zija has been around for around for about 5 years and therefore it's not brand new and risky, it has been established just long enough to be a fantastic opportunity. In 5 short years, it has really shot out of the starting gate.

A "ground floor" opportunity is defined as under 300,000 distributers. If a company has less than 150,000 distributers it's considered a "once in a lifetime opportunity" according to network marketing professionals. Now although this company is approaching that coveted 150k mark fast, that is worldwide. At the time of writing this book there are only about 70,000 active distributers in the USA and Canada only has around 7,000! Talk about timing!

So this is the perfect timing to get on board whether you are in the west or in the east because with this global opportunity you can build a team from home that consists of distributers in any active country!

Once again, I say, as I did in my introduction, I am NOT a Zija distributer. Nor are any of my relatives. I now have met many Zija product users and seen the difference in their lives. It's amazing. So, I can say, without anyone suggesting I profit should you join the rest of the Zija team, it would be well worth your time and energy. Each of us is going to hear about Zija, and it's going to happen with or without you. Might as well be with you.

The product is unbelievable and is 100% natural, making every person on the planet a potential customer, the 6 month old baby, the breastfeeding wife, her mother, the professional kickboxing trainer, even your Grandma will all want and NEED this tremendous product! No other company can make the claim! Zija's product is based in the miracle plant called Moringa Oleifera and it is grown, not created synthetically in a lab, so our bodies absorb 100% of it!

The pay plan and all of their training is definitely second to none so that part of the equation is covered. Each person is rewarded by helping the team with team bonuses among and other financial benefits. Soon, you will be at a point where the Zija will cover your product cost and eventually provide you with a Mercedes Benz to call your own.

Lastly the support on this team is phenomenal! You will have access to an amazing organization of people that have helped push, pull and drag each other to the top, teamwork and support is really not to be undervalued here because it's really the difference between sinking and swimming. You aren't looking to sink are you? With this company, if you do the work, you will excel.

"Zija International" has created so many financially independent people in its first five years and is just now in its "momentum" stage where the company will double and double and double in size very quickly. Wouldn't you like to sneak in before the boom?

Now is your opportunity. I encourage you to do your research by trying the product "Moringa Oleifera" and if you have any questions contact the first person who suggested you look at Zija. They will do their best to answer any questions you have and help you get started.

One last word of advice. If Zija is your business choice, play for keeps. You are going to come across others in different networking opportunities, and they will want you to join with them. There is nothing wrong with other companies per se, but if you wish to make REAL life long income, keep your head down, keep to your plan, and tell the Zija story. It's not important that they buy your story, it's important that you don't buy theirs. You'll end up regretting it.

Further, if you have a Zija product story, or a business testimonial, I'd love to hear about it. Send me a quick email and I'll follow up with you. Maybe you will be in the next edition of this book! Now that would be a help in creating your credibility! See below for more details.

Max Hailey

A note on testimonials found in this book:

Each person who made these testimonials did so freely. No testimonial was paid for by the author, publisher, or anyone connected to this book. I have edited them for space and readability, but not in any factual way. My researcher collected these testimonials, and FYI, none of the people knew they would be in this book, nor did they have any other connection to this book. There are literally thousands of people who are now leading healthy lives thanks to Zija.

A special and important note:

Even after extensive research, I am always open to more views. If you have a Zija story to tell about how the product has changed your life or health, please send me your story. If you have a business success story, I welcome it too. My publisher will be updating both the Kindle and Paper versions of this book weekly, and your story can be in the book. Email me at Max.Hailey@AllAmericanISP.com . By sending me your story, you give me the right to publish it. I may edit it for readability.

My research on Zija and those associated with it has made me truly appreciate the amazing opportunity that it provides. It is just in its infancy, here in 2013, and I predict it to become a major dominate contributor to health, wellness and prosperity for those who are smart enough to commit themselves to spreading the word about Zija.

If you enjoyed this book, please leave an honest review on Amazon. Reviews help others find books that interest them, and help authors do a better job in their next book. If you enjoyed this book and have an interest in Zija, leaving a review here can help spread the word about your Zija story. Feel free to add your product story to the review – by putting in your product story as well as the review of the book you spread the word on Zija. Put in your full name if you wish, it will be there for your prospects to see when they search you out and consider you as an upline. It builds your social presence.

If you have constructive suggestions, please write to me at the email above.

I wish each and every one of you a full and abundant life – be healthy and wealthy!

Max.

Made in the USA
Lexington, KY
10 February 2014